Poetry Ireland Review 124

Eagarthóir / Editor
EAVAN BOLAND

© Poetry Ireland Ltd 2018

Poetry Ireland Ltd / Éigse Éireann Teo gratefully acknowledges the assistance of The Arts Council / An Chomhairle Ealaíon and The Arts Council of Northern Ireland.

LOTTERY FUNDED

Poetry Ireland invites individuals and commercial organizations to become Friends of Poetry Ireland. For more details, please contact:

Poetry Ireland Friends Scheme, Poetry Ireland, 11 Parnell Square East, Dublin 1, Ireland

or telephone +353 1 6789815; e-mail info@poetryireland.ie

FRIENDS:
Joan and Joe McBreen, Desmond Windle, Neville Keery,
Noel and Anne Monahan, Ruth Webster, Maurice Earls,
Mary Shine Thompson, Seán Coyle, Henry and Deirdre Comerford,
Thomas Dillon Redshaw, Rachel Joynt, Helen Flanagan, Maura Hanlon,
Eithne Hand, William McConkey, Andrew Caldicott

ISBN: 978-1-902121-71-0
ISSN: 0332-2998

PUBLICATIONS MANAGER: **Paul Lenehan**, with the assistance of **Supriya Dhaliwal** and **Koryne Martinez**

IRISH-LANGUAGE EDITOR: **Caitlín Nic Íomhair**

DESIGN: **Alistair Keady (www.hexhibit.com)**

COVER CREDIT: 'Iconic IV' by **Aisling Conroy**

Contents

Editorial

This issue contains, first of all, the continuing vitality of new voices and recent poems. This has been one of the privileges of editing for me. I never get tired of the surprise and variety involved in reading these poems and being able to provide a presence for some of them in this review.

Also here, two views of the city of Dublin through its history and its poets: Adam Hanna's fine essay 'Thomas Kinsella: The Civil Servant-Poet at Mid-Century' is paired with a fascinating glimpse of that time in the poet's own words, through a short interview he did with Hanna.

Kinsella's retrospect reveals him as a working writer at the heart of government in the 1950s. His time in the Department of Finance as TK Whitaker's private secretary allowed him a rare access to an evolving Ireland: "Dealing with the annual budget," he says "it was possible to see the functioning of the entire economy." As a poet whose storied poems of Dublin helped to define the city in Irish poetry, this is a rare and precious recollection of the outer life that went with that inner one.

Paula Meehan's sequence, 'Museum', uncovers another city. It was commissioned by the Tenement Museum project at Henrietta Street. She gave an early reading there, when the project was just commencing. In Charles Duggan's after-note – he is the Dublin City Council Heritage Officer and was involved in commissioning the sequence – he states: "Her words resonated within the crumbling walls of this house as we set out to recover its histories and memories." In the same way, the powerful poems in 'Museum' map a poignant and important journey from lives to language.

Alice Kinsella is the featured poet. Her new book *Flower Press*, published in February by The Onslaught Press, follows a path of elegy – the work in her own words 'written through a cloud of regret and grief'. The poems included here are spirited disclosures, ready to come to the threshold of the surreal but also intimate and present in language.

Finally, a two-fold discussion of the recently published *The Cambridge Companion to Irish Poets*. Fiona Sampson's thoughtful review offers one perspective. The eloquent counter-statement – drawn from Chris Murray's excellent Poethead website – provides another, one which weighs the effect of excluding essential women's voices from this volume. The statement represents a convergence of women poets and academics from both the north and south of Ireland, who 'felt a response to the gender imbalance in *The Cambridge Companion to Irish Poets* was necessary'. Their argument is compelling. To start with, it's evident that such a book cannot be presented in the classroom as inclusive or authoritative – an effect Cambridge University Press can hardly have intended. But there are wider effects. It's also clear, as this statement suggests, that absences distort presences. If past achievement is erased, present achievement can only exist in a flawed context. For any editor, that's a case to answer.

– Eavan Boland

Colm Brennan

MINDFULNESS

Don't tell me about silence.
Don't tell me you made yourself sit
cross-legged on the bedroom floor.
You gotta just be, you know? Don't say it.
Without your phone, like, truly alone.
Don't tell me about living in the moment.
Don't tell me the bloody alarm bleeps when
ten minutes of being present have expired?

I already know what it's like. To lie in a darkened room
with nothing but my life to distract me. To stomp
over the slippery leaves and resilient needles
of a forest floor on a crisp November morning
and peer past bare branches at the bright grey sky.

And I know what it's like to wait in line,
wipe someone's breath from a tram window
and hurry, forcing a path through the throngs,
just in case, god-forbid, I miss my stop.
Don't tell me I *should* try it sometime.

Faye Boland

TOO LATE

By the time the seas are clogged with plastic
and the last fish has gasped its final breath
it will be too late to save the seagulls

who starved to death, gullets obstructed
by shards of plastic. Too late for the seals,
smothered by bags and six-pack rings.

Small-fry voices protest, swim against
the current. No space
to breathe.

By the time the tide turns
it will be too late to save the dodo,
butchered into extinction by sailors,

the Tasmanian tiger and the baiji dolphin.
And no-one will remember the noble elk
who wandered our forests

or the lonely howl
of the last wolf
before she fell.

Ciarán O'Rourke

ROS INBHIR

Let the sky-thin seasons stake their claim

in the ditch of my eyes,
in the flood of my bones,
in the torn out root of my mouth –

I'll move
like light in the dirt, or a lifting lark,
like rain at the edge of your meadowed mind.

Daniel Lusk

PALIMPSEST

Said the father came to her bed
and the gibbous moon appeared
in the frame of the window
with her apron, her wimple and beads

said she was the sacrifice
she was the lamb
in its perfume of hawthorn flowers
and the witness spoke not

appeared out of nothing, a shadow
and the witness moon spoke not

a weight, an invisible bloom
stinking of rank Fritillaria
said god is love
said this is what love is.

but the nightjar saw and the crickets told
and the lion in the mountain screamed.

Now is the bed of never,
the room and the door of forgetting.
And didn't she wake there
to the weightless moon and its lightness.
Wake to the blood.

Jimmy O'Connell

HARBOUR STREET, TULLAMORE

Here are Sunday afternoon shoppers where another
time ago the silence of religious observation
hung penitentially, or, on occasion, a club

match in O'Connor Park might see a procession of men,
cigarettes in hand, nervously anticipating
county glory. I smell petrol fumes now, but also there,

in the air, unexpectedly, the smell of animal
piss, that clean sharp tang must have seeped into
these stones and cement grooved paths, released

now to stagger memory into life: calves slipping
and slithering down green urine slopped trailers;
pigs, pink and manure slathered, squealing in riotous

protest as farmers, nicotine fingered, Wellingtons
stuffed with brown stained dungarees, turn
and twist them into display. Smell has tricked me

into hearing my Grandmother, sending me to
Wrafters for a pound and a half of back rashers,
"And make sure he gives you Tullamore sausages."

He still stands there behind the counter, flour dust
in his hair, slicing bacon; the smell of stale Guinness
lingering from behind the yellow glass frosted door.

"You too will be a memory like me, young fella."
He wraps the sausages in grease paper, "Others will
remember you for the ordinary ould things."

Julie Morrissy

CONSTRUCTING OUR-SELVES

Hannah Sullivan, *Three Poems* (Faber and Faber, 2018), £10.99.
Annemarie Ní Churreáin, *Bloodroot* (Doire Press, 2017), €12.
Emma McKervey, *The Rag Tree Speaks* (Doire Press, 2017), €12.

In her debut *Three Poems*, Hannah Sullivan joins the long-form tradition
with confidence, ambition, and style. 'You, Very Young in New York'
opens the collection, immediately reflecting upon the repetitive nature of
time. The phrase 'nothing happens' appears twice on the first page as Sullivan delicately weaves through scenes from a young woman's life,
apparently lacking in purpose. The poem conveys a sense of pointless-
ness, testing the veracity of our connections in commerce, social media,
global and urban life. One passage reads, '… and hipsters / Keep on trying to sell huckleberry jam from Brooklyn and novelists / Keep on going to
Starbucks to craft their sagas, adjusting their schemas, / Picking like pigeons
at the tail of the morning croissant'. In one continuous movement, the
first poem explores the 'saga' of our lives in a digital, capitalist world full
of camera phones, Negronis, and 'The beige Lego-maze of offices'. While
contemplating a man in Chennai, 'Checking the cricket scores on his
computer, reading Thoreau, / Wondering what New York looks like at
night, in snow', Sullivan articulates the prevailing challenge of the collection: 'an attempt to live deliberately'. These poems consistently ask how
we can meaningfully engage in the context of our hyper-connected moment,
while at the same time drawing on the rich history of the modernist long
poem.
     The bromidic atmosphere continues in the individually numbered
units of the second poem, 'Repeat Until Time / The Heraclitus Poem':

> But, forever fumbling for the snooze button, the gym is there
> Forever, and the teeth silt over yellow to be flossed, and there
> Will be, in eternity, coffee to be brewed and that moment in the shower
> When you open your mouth and rhotacise the water and just stand there,
> Stupid bliss of hot water, tongue-tingling, steaming the shower.

In these lines, and throughout the collection, Sullivan delves deeper than
simple hopelessness. While her poetry certainly embodies the inevitability
of routine, at the same time she manages to reveal true moments; that
second in time where something as simple as opening your mouth in the
shower connects you to life and to living more than any of the devices or
interactions you will encounter during your day. Sullivan invests in those

moments – when we feel the weight and joy of life, death, birth, and dailiness.

The collection ends with 'The Sandpit After Rain', reflecting upon the birth of Sullivan's son and the death of her father. '2. Hospital Windowsills' is a refreshingly candid poem recounting an overdue pregnancy, Caesarean section, and the first days and hours with a new baby. The poem reveals the underlying complexity in the ceremony of life events, particularly those moments when we think we should feel a certain way.

> The baby did not look like my father at all,
> But there was a resemblance:
> Our slight awkwardness with each other.
>
> Neither of us was at our best, that first night
>   – '3. WHEN THE EGG MEETS THE WHISK'

These poems express a resilience and desire to really live in the bizarre conditions we have assented to, perhaps suggesting that through the act of living, we can rebel against going through the motions.

Annemarie Ní Churreáin's debut, *Bloodroot*, opens with an untitled poem, setting up questions that run throughout the collection. The speaker of 'Untitled' – 'I was thirteen and only spoke a weave of ordinary tongues' – is emerging from girlhood into a complex world in which she must find her place. The poem closes, '*Come underground*, they said. / *See what we are made of*', a call that lurks throughout the collection's three parts. In exploring this call, Ní Churreáin draws together notions of place and landscape, both as physical sites of discovery but also as sites that build a collective imaginary of our origins, particularly as women. Ní Churreáin balances herself between these elements in her poetic investigation into precisely what we are made of.

Part I is a journey through childhood and family, with poems such as 'The Lane', 'Sisters', and 'Ball Game with Ruby Aged 5' nostalgically reflecting on schooldays, rebellion, and play. This part is also spiked with poems alluding to the more serious themes developed later in the collection. The title poem 'Bloodroot', written at Castlepollard Mother and Baby Home, begins an investigation into the lived experiences of women in Ireland, asking 'Were you made to kneel here too, Mary, Josephine, Bernadette? / If I call you by your house-names will you speak?'. The collection hits its stride in Part II, particularly the first seven poems. A confidence emerges, with Ní Churreáin confronting issues of gender-based oppression in Ireland with poise and wary inquisitiveness. Many of these poems explicitly reference Mother and Baby Homes, and Ní Churreáin dedicates 'The Secret' to Ann Lovett, the 15-year-old girl who died giving birth beside a grotto in Co Longford in 1984. 'The Kerry Foot' and 'Saidhbhín' are the strongest poems in the collection, carefully blending poetic image, delicate subjectivity, and a hard connection to reality. The protesting spirit invoked in 'Newborn, 1984' is as relevant now as it was then, and Ní Churreáin's image of Mary Manning refusing 'to pass an orange through / the check-out / at a Dunnes Stores desk' stayed with me long after I read the poem.

The move from childhood in Part I to the serious issues of Part II builds a subtle arc into the collection. Part III opens with 'Laundry', set in India, and it also features poems set in Tibet, Goa, and Florida. The more personally reflective tone of Part III perhaps moves somewhat briskly away from the deep contemplation of structural oppression in Part II. However, the collection ends with the brilliant and evocative 'Market Prayer', a poem that lyrically reunites the overall themes of the collection, and gestures towards a future – for the poet, for women, and perhaps for poetry in general:

> Pomona of Orchards, please:
> like the finder of a planet
> seeing for the first time
> an otherness, I am afraid
> the life I dream exists.

Ní Churreáin leaves the reader in her carefully constructed world of considered hope, always mindful of the events that have led us to our present, but daring to reach further, collectively and as individuals.

Emma McKervey's debut *The Rag Tree Speaks* blends lyric subjectivity with nature, history, language, and mythology, introducing a careful eye for the exquisite. Many of these poems densely stack detail, investigating typical elements of our landscape such as gorse, turf, and seaweed in order to reveal fresh insights on contemporary life. Her ekphrastic poem, 'Mad Red', places the speaker at the centre of the familiar site of the bog, responding to artist Paul Henry's 'The Potato Diggers'. A parallel is drawn between the woman in Henry's painting, dressed in traditional red, and McKervey's assertion, 'I am Mad Red in the bog', as her stumble disturbs the surrounding nature. The speaker stands in the 'moss stew' and contemplates a complex sense of self in the midst of the landscape, memories of her childhood, and a glimpse of the family cottage in the distance, pushing against but ultimately acknowledging that self is constructed alongside these elements:

> ... and I want to find the thing
> that will take me out of myself
> but instead realise I have always been Mad Red.

McKervey encounters nature with poise and inquisitiveness in poems such as 'Cedar Wood', 'Wren', 'Bullfinch', and 'Beyond the Mussel Banks'. However, the collection also explores ordinary moments in human relationships. In 'Ex-Lovers' Car Boot Sale', she writes about the consumable debris of people's lives, and in 'Best Years' she reflects on motherhood, with the speaker recounting days in her twenties spent pushing prams, going to bed early, and 'watching roundabouts / go round and round'. At its best, the collection plays on these cyclical rhythms of life through a poetics that is injected with fact, trivia, and reference to historical and cultural events. Language too represents rich ground in the poems. The collection opens with 'An Sciathán', and considers the lack of specific Irish words for 'hand' or 'foot'. The benevolence of language crops up again in 'Ernest Wilson Goes to China', 'The Pithos Jar', and 'Patagonia'. McKervey takes on a breadth of topics in this collection, which, comprising sixty-four poems, is more extensive than many debuts. Perhaps, the thematic links throughout would be strengthened if the collection were shorter. However, McKervey builds a distinct sensibility over the course of the collection, registering her struggle with ideas of home, nation, and womanhood, bringing these themes to life with a gentle poetic gaze.

Stanley Conn

THE ENEMY

Afraid, bewildered
Gathering her children round
While the mob spits and snarls
Packing up a few belongings
Knowing the rest will be pilfered
Or trashed

Put out by the neighbours
In Belfast, in Bosnia, in Beirut
Whom she lived amongst
Was friends to
Chatted to
Passed time in the street with
Joked with

Taigs Out
Moslem Scum
Christian Blasphemers

Words daubed on the walls
Faces contorted with hate
And fear
Well meaning people, decent people
Just seeking out the enemy

Simon Ó Faoláin

FÁSACH
– do Nuala Ní Dhómhnaill

'Gus in ainneoin gach a bhfuil agam,
de dheargainneoin saol na míne,
Tá an aisling thréan im' intinn.

Tá clochán in airde ar chliathán na Screige
– Díon fós ina sheasamh idir spéir agus talamh –
a dhéanfadh cúis.

Labhraíonn an fiach go bráthardha ann,
ritheann giorria i gcoinne fána,
Dónn an fheadóg bhuí mar ghríos.

Ní bheadh iomairí pónairí agam ann,
(Tá's ag madraí an bhaile nach bhfásann
pónairí ar oileán ná ar shliabh gan fothain),

Mhairfinn ar fhraocháin, rútaí brioscláin, fuilig,
Agus b'fhéidir buidéal *Laphroaig*
i dtaisce in almóir an chlocháin.

Bheadh braon agam tráthnóntaí breátha,
Suite idir ursain an dorais ag féachaint
ar ghrian na fola thar Shliabh an Iolair.

Do-scartha ó dheatach na móna sa bholgam
bheadh blas na ndroichead dóite uilig,
Is ná cuirfeadh san aon mhairg orm.

Marion McCready

I DID NOT KNOW YOU, MONIACK MHOR

but you have always been there
in one guise or another.
I trace the range of Strathfarrar
    with my finger,
I draw the line of it in the air.

There is no sea, no sea here,
no *Juno, Jupiter* or *Saturn*
(the ships of my childhood).

At Moniack Mhor I lie with the bees,
their still bodies floating above me.
A horse rider clips in the lower valley,
    curlews cry in my ear.

Hills fall behind hills,
behind hills. Moniack Mhor
is forever opening –
a gift of dry grass, crab clouds,
the green nest of furze slowly breaking apart.

Nightly the yellow almond buds
    creep closer,
until I can taste them in the dark air.

Jean Tuomey

GIFT

I give you our view,
our Sunday afternoon one
from the top of Ben Gorm.
It will last longer than a photo,
will never fade.
Take it out of your coat pocket on rainy days,
keep it in an inner one.

Turn around in a full circle,
it's all yours;

the steep hill we climbed,
the flat stone where you sat, waited for me,
the sheep who called to their lambs,
the lake in the distance, tipped by the horizon,
the turf already footed by the friendly farmer,
and best of all,
the safe descent home.

Jessica Traynor

FABULOUS BEASTS

Alison Hackett, *crabbing* (21st Century Renaissance, 2017), €18.
Amanda Bell, *first the feathers* (Doire Press, 2017), €12.
Rosie Shepperd, *The Man At The Corner Table* (Seren Books, 2015), £9.99.

The debut collection is often a composite creature; a mythological hybrid of sorts, the result of a decade or so of poetic meanderings and experiment. When they are successful, they have the savage beauty of a sphinx or a chimera; this is balanced by the risk that the work could turn out neither fish nor fowl. These three collections all bear the hallmarks of the debut, containing poems on themes of universal relevance: love affairs (failed or successful), the death of beloved parents, and childhood memories. They all explore the use of form to give these familiar themes a fresh gloss. The mark of success in these instances is whether a fresh and engaging voice emerges to imbue these universal themes with a particular life and energy.

Crabbing by Alison Hackett is a first collection which deals almost exclusively with a childhood trauma, the sudden death of the poet's mother. This is a collection written with a sense of urgency, seeking catharsis. The first part of the collection deals with the discovery of the poet's mother's death, establishing the secure world of home before demonstrating its disintegration. Hackett displays a talent for simple but effective poetic language, capturing the sights and sounds of her childhood life with an unshowy precision that helps to convey the emotional depth of her experience. In 'Rocky Bay', a child's bewilderment at her mother's funeral is captured in the plaintive lines:

> In the evening the fire is lit, curtains drawn
> the hum and murmur of the crowd
> chicken fricassée and rice is served.
> It smells like a party.

An instinct for plucking a seemingly quotidian moment from memory and allowing it to speak volumes is also demonstrated in 'Fisherman's Friend', where a sick friend's pausing to eat the eponymous sweet becomes a telling moment of vulnerability: 'a sweet to keep him breathing / through the five miles ahead'.

Richer detail abounds in the book's title poem, 'Crabbing', which zooms in on a happy childhood memory:

> We head out in the clinker built punt,
> salt and dirt and streaks of rotten wood
> trapped in its layers of varnish.
> The seagull engine putters out its beat –
> a staccato morse code message
> of our journey out to sea.

Hackett captures the music of the sea in these lines, but tempers any potential sentimentality with the introduction of an adult awareness of the crab's fate: 'They froth and bubble in the choking air'.

Hackett outlines the poems' biographical context in an introduction, a rather unusual convention in a poetry book, and I felt a little cheated of the opportunity to discover the poet's experiences through the poetry itself. There are moments in this collection where the drive to achieve catharsis can threaten to overwhelm editorial considerations, meaning that some poems don't quite achieve the freshness of those detailed above. However, as a testament to a child's grief, *Crabbing* succeeds in its poetic aims.

If *Crabbing* is selkie-like in its engagement with a coastal landscape, Amanda Bell's *first the feathers* is an airborne beast, its reflections on life, love, and death threaded through with bird motifs and imagery. This is a tactile collection which doesn't shy away from the visceral. The title poem finds the poet plucking and gutting a woodcock, the action of which prompts an uneasy juxtaposition with more tender actions: 'though I can't erase the trace / of talcum-powdered belly / from my fingers'.

The collection contemplates harm, both accidental and institutional. A number of poems deal with events such as the death of Savita Halappanavar and make reference to the burials at Tuam, or the death of Joanne Hayes, either obliquely or directly. It's certainly refreshing to see a thirst for public and political engagement in a debut, but also quite a challenge to make an original poetic statement on these events, which have been dealt with in some very well-known Irish poems. Bell's method of setting her work apart involves an ambitious formal approach, and she makes skilful use of haibun, ballad, villanelle, ghazal, and sestina. Of these, the haibun are perhaps the most successful, serving to demarcate the various sections of the collection and to reinforce its central themes. The image of a rotting gannet disintegrating in the poet's hands in 'So Long' is particularly memorable.

Also noteworthy, among the formal poems, is 'The Ballad of Mary Anne Cadden', an impressive retelling of the story of the infamous backstreet abortionist. The ballad form seems well-suited to this particular tale, creating unusual tonal contrasts, and although the requirements of metre can mean that some lines feel a little padded-out, the starkness of the form works to convey the shock factor of the story:

Charged with child abandonment, Mamie was sent to prison –
The guards went in to search her house and dug up the back garden.

Although they found a foetus there no charge was ever brought –
'Twas only for the living child she came before the court.

Plus ça change, the reader may well think. This collection looks at child-birth and rearing from a number of different angles, and Bell is particularly strong when juxtaposing the joyful physicality of this experience with loss. In 'Phantom', she meditates on a friend's experience of a mastectomy and her own memories of breast feeding. The poem's final stanza riffs on Larkin's 'An Arundel Tomb', culminating in a line suffused with aching sadness:

If an amputated limb continues itching,
and a missing breast still tenses in the chill,
I fear that what survives of us may not, in fact,
be love, but a disembodied longing to be held.

From one airborne collection to another, Rosie Shepperd's *The Man at the Corner Table* is perhaps the best travelled of our fantastical creatures; a cosmopolitan sphinx of a collection. Shepperd's is a unique and confident voice which delights in the surreal, and although we find ourselves again in the territory of love and loss, we've seldom viewed the terrain from this angle. In 'it's not just the underfloor heating that makes me lie down in the kitchen', the poet literally takes to the kitchen floor in an attempt to find a position which might make life bearable, 'even though I know the dog / will try to lick my face and / even though crystals of mouse bait lie / blue and a yard from my nose'.

This is a collection which tempers loss with humour in a manner that is always refreshing and surprising. These are poems which feature trap-doors into unexpected new landscapes. A quick wit means the poems are often spiky, but never devoid of empathy, and the reader often finds themselves moved by a deft change in tone. In 'What I need, Bernard, is a bit of notice;', the speaker tersely demands a little consideration from her unresponsive partner when planning his imminent funeral: 'I don't have a preference and it is your funeral. / I just wish, / I wish we had longer to look at the menus.' This funny litany is exploded later in the poem, as the poet blind-sides us with a moment of intimacy:

Bernard?
I'm going to hold your hand now.
This is like the old days. Remember the picnics?

You always forged ahead with your spy-nocs to find the perfect spot,
said you wouldn't risk detritus spoiling our cold cuts.

Your hands were always fresh and cool,
rather like ham, Bernard, rather like
a nice tinned ham.

Shepperd's eye for minute but meaningful details, and her ability to balance pathos and bathos, are again demonstrated in 'Lump', a poem that deals with an ungainly and neglected teenager. It's a rare talent to be able to address a tragic situation with such clear-eyed wit, and the wry sadness of the poem's final line echoes in the reader's mind:

Last month he ran onto platform 11, towards an Intercity and into

a ticket attendant from St Lucia who provided a small sweet cup
of polystyrene tea, a telephone number and enough soothing
silence. Poor lump, I should not know this about you, but I do.
I know this about you and you know I know and I know you do.

Shepperd's poems loop and unravel across the page, and many of their titles serve as the poem's first line. This approach helps to unpack the density of Shepperd's vision, which at times can take a little time for the reader to access. However, these poems are full of rewards and each of their composite parts – their lion's mane, their serpent's tail – is a thing of beauty in and of itself.

Each of these three collections merits further exploration than time or space will allow here; this, again, is the challenge of commenting on debuts which have clearly been many years in the making. It will be interesting to see how these fantastical creatures evolve – whether they choose to settle, daemon-like, into one form, or to maintain their composite nature over the course of collections to come.

Paula Meehan

MUSEUM

Invocation

As old houses harbour ghosts, so do words.
Take *museum* which comes down from the Greek,
a place to put things that please the Muses,

a shrine or seat of the old goddesses.
What you find here might not be what you seek.
Rich, poor, citizen, commoner, lady, lord:

mortal trace made immortal by design.
Surrender as you enter through their door;
know all are equal here: in Time's brute trust

we are held – the quick, the dead, the blest, the curst.
Open heart and mind to those who've gone before,
to honour the Muses – virgin, mother, crone,

and hope to glimpse them ninefold in this house,
daughters of Memory, oracles of grace.

OF NATAL CHARTS AND END GAMES
to Urania – Muse of Astronomy

Not the clock to measure time and tide, but the moon,
her waxings, her wanings, her track across the star-
spangled heavens, trining and sextiling planets
to net and land another whole incarnate soul,
to earth this karma in the shelter of the house.
Cellular mirrors celestial, the spinning globe
slows to rest with the mother's cries, the child's first breath;

while elsewhere in the house, a different room, a death,
a last glimpse of ceiling as the light fails lobe by lobe.
Upstairs someone dreams of walnuts, a new blouse,
someone makes coddle, snuffs a candle, humps coal,
sips Vartry water, tastes trace of phyllite, quartzite,
greywacke, shale, slate – bedrock lithographies from far-
off Wicklow – while Angelus bells ring out the noon.

HER DIGNITY: A RESTORATION
to Clio – Muse of History

Once it was simple and clear: the world a dreamspace
when we were children and wrote in our copybooks
an old penny, an old hat, an old watch, an old boot,
an old house tells its story. An old woman tells *hers*
now, walking backwards into the future, her eyes
wide open, peering through the air so thick with trauma,
to the girl she once was, skipping the shadowy world

into being with each thump of the rope, or curled
to a foetal crouch under the bed, adult drama
raging overhead. You, who write the histories,
write her in, write her up, write her down, before she blurs,
an image disturbed in a scrying bowl, that the brute
erosions of a State helmed by liars, helmed by crooks,
might not yet rob memory of her abiding grace.

CHILDREN OF THE WIND
to Euterpe – Muse of Song and Elegiac Poetry

Where are they now, the children of the house, who flocked
like rooks at dust, or gulls come in from stormy seas,
raucous through the rooms, from area up to attic
to nest in cribs, to huddle in beds, to dream in cots,
to rise again in the morning, to make the whole
world up, over and over, their voices piping,
puling, shrilling, in glorious cacophony?

They had no fear of time. Their ancient cartographies
still scribed in the walls, their seeking, their hiding,
their yo-yos, their piggy beds, their ludo, their … goals!
"I'm coming, ready or not, keep your place or you'll be caught".
Their rhyming chants echo even yet. O my erratic
stars, that wandered the face of the heavens,
blown hither, blown thither, on cosmic currents rocked.

THE ACOUSTIC
to Erato – Muse of Lyric Poetry

As slowly as a tortoise, time moves through these rooms:
light eternal nuzzling up to windows and under doors,
ethereal music – a voice broken with desire
that plucks at the heartstrings. It sings of love, love lost
and hope abandoned. It sings of an empty bed,
of roses and myrtle withering in a glass jar,
of turtle doves, of snow falling to the garden.

They were much like us: they lived, they died on the margin.
The archive opens, a glimpse of who they were, star-
crossed lovers. Then slams shut again on the silenced dead.
We fare no better now than they once did – the cost
of love for some frail souls is a funeral pyre.
We'll keep on making songs, we'll sing through peace, through war,
our songs of lovers lonely in their vaulted tombs.

'STEP WE GAILY, ON WE GO'
to Terpsichore – Muse of Dance

Some nights when the moon is full the ghosts come out to dance:
they reel and they jig and they jitter across the boards.
They clasp each other's spectral hands throughout the ages,
Republican shimmies with Ascendancy lady,
Militia Captain toe to toe with scullery maid.
They swing their partners while spirit music blares;
sage, fool, rich, poor, made equal in this Danse Macabre.

A rustle of silk, a rattle of tarnished sabre,
their shadowy shindig teeming up the backstairs
to trip the light fandango, beau and jade,
skeletal revenants grieving the loss of body,
remembering strong hearts pounding in rib cages,
blood rising, pulsing with the music's major chords
to possess the frenzied dancers in ecstatic trance.

THIS BED, THIS RAFT ON STORMY SEAS
to Melpomene – Muse of Tragedy

The start of her lying-in was the end of mornings
at the pier glass, mouse-skin eyebrows, eyes outlined in jet,
cheeks rouged, got from recipes in *The Art of Beauty*;
gall-nuts, black lead, mercury, carmine, liquid pitch,
her glued on beauty spots of taffeta and silk,
her drapery, her napery, her blue, blue, walls.
Birth the leveller pays no heed to class, to kind –

our crossing fraught with peril to body and to mind.
In every generation there are stars that fall;
a lost galaxy of nurture with our mother's milk;
a miracle we make it here without a hitch.
This buzzing hive of life, this golden bounty,
honey of survival in our ancestors' sweat,
salt tears for those who don't survive the quickening.

OF ODYSSEYS AND OTHER RAMBLES
to Calliope – Muse of Epic Poetry

Yap yap! Ráiméis and rigmarole! If these walls could speak:
Hentown blather clucked from threshold to attic room,
fabrications, downright lies, home truths and lullabies.
Story snagged from time, spun into the yarn of the house,
the ghostly racket of the carriers of tales
who lug their water buckets up and down the stairs,
all gossip, all frittery bustle, their epic.

If musing on the ornamental frieze of oak,
an iridescent bird through a canopy of air
lets drop a feather to your hand, then use it as a quill
to enumerate such fates, damned or auspicious;
the census of this shelter might immortalize
such vestige of lives endured through crash, through boom,
flitting like some magpie, stolen trinket in her beak.

Funny Ha Ha And Funny Peculiar
to Thalia – Muse of Comedy

Laughter, they say, is nature's best medicine:
through thick and thin, through paucity and plenty,
with your glass half empty, with your glass half full,
if you have a glass, a pot to piss in, a jam jar,
a fork when it's raining soup, when god slams one door
in your face, then locks the other door and bars the window –
you'd have to laugh, or else you'd break down and cry.

It's hard to take the cosmic joke when kids are hungry,
when the cupboard is bare and the fuel's running low;
sniggers, guffaws, snorts, pratfalls and gallows humour.
Is it funny ha ha or funny peculiar
when one by one neighbours take ill, are listless, eyes dull?
Words like typhoid, diphtheria, rickets and dysentery
wipe the smile off your face, invite terror creep in.

Our Lady Of The Apocalypse
to Polyhymnia – Muse of Sacred Poetry

Our Lady of the apocalypse who never
closed your heart to the dissolute, pray for us
who gave shelter in broken down Georgian tenements,
who kept the doors open to the demented ones,
those who came in rags and miasmas of foul odour,
in delirium tremens, the worn out old spunkers,
the displaced relics of imperial trauma.

O sweet daughter of Memory, veiled in enigma,
who brought longed for oblivion to the meths drinkers,
the dipsos, the alcos, the put down no hopers,
those who came in from chaos, from cold, from winds, from rains,
to sleep it all off in hallways, in stairwells, who rent
the long night with sobs, who cried out to you in the throes
of their last agony, grant them eternal succour.

Envoi

THE DAUGHTERS OF MEMORY

They're hanging out the sheets on the lines
to catch a spring wind. The children dream
of schooners under a cloud of sail
and the ghosts are packing up their satchels.

They know it's time to leave, with the tide
of history ebbing through the house.

Go you too, mortal, your fated road.
May fixed stars guide you, until you reach
safe harbour, a place you can call home.

– Therma, Ikaria, Greece, 22.5.2017

In July 2015, in 14 Henrietta St, Paula Meehan gave an emotion-
ally powerful reading of her poem 'The Pattern' (from *The Man
Who Was Marked by Winter*), to open a research colloquium at the
beginning stages of the Tenement Museum Dublin project. Her words
resonated within the crumbling walls of this house as we set out to
recover its histories and memories, and to begin the restoration of its
fragile rooms and the creation of the Tenement Museum. The poem's
image of Paula's mother, who scrubbed the floor 'an armreach at a time',
then buffed and shined it, is the memory of all the mothers who lived
within the walls of 14 Henrietta St. Nearly two years later, our initial
research completed, Paula was invited to consider the house's complex
social and cultural history – eighteenth-century townhouse, tenement
house, museum – and to create new poetic works in response. What
has emerged is 'Museum', a collection of eleven poems, dedicated to
the nine muses, giving voice to memories of mothers, childhood, and
domestic life, across the centuries. The poems, published for the first
time in this issue of *Poetry Ireland Review*, will form part of the museum's
exhibitions and audio tours.

Charles Duggan,
Heritage Officer, and Project Director, Tenement Museum Dublin
www.tenementmuseum.ie/

Tony O'Dwyer

NAMING THE DEAD

Here is a listing of the dead,
Each name chased by the mason's broach
In swashed curlicues;
The Greeks believed that stone dissolved the flesh,
And so we think of them lying in a house of decay,
Strewn with chips of coffin-wood and rust-pocked nails,
Their gnarled fingers crossed,
Their naked bones curling in the walled-up dark.

But imagine them gathered round the piano
Of an evening in draped and lamplit rooms:
Pale hands I loved beside the Shalimar,
Where are you now? Who lies beneath your spell?
Or sitting at a door in summer,
Hay bleaching in all the meadows,
The evening air filled with lush accretions,
Gazing along the valley fields
To where Mount Callan rises
Like the blue wall of the world.
Beyond it Europe weeps;
Famine ships are sailing; Whitman rests
His pen from *Leaves of Grass*;
Morse is tapping out *What hath God wrought*;
The wagon trains go west.

This is the enigma of the dead:
To live in memory, come back in dreams,
Insist we honour them with stones,
Call out their names, letter after letter,
To hammer-ring and chisel-chase;
We leave them limestone,
Promises to sing for them in chantries.
Siste, viator they say, over and over, *Siste, viator.*

Fiona Sampson

TRAPPED INSIDE HISTORY

Edited by Gerald Dawe, *The Cambridge Companion to Irish Poets* (Cambridge University Press, 2017), £26.99.

Give it another fifty years, and readers will look back at 2018 and see nothing surprising about the small number of women who appear in today's literary anthologies. Just like us when we look back half a century, they will view these as laughably primitive times, a period before women had equal rights in employment or reproduction, when society still policed its young women in such particular ways that only rare exceptions could make it through the barrier of expectations to the intellectual and creative freedom that being a writer – and being an excellent writer in particular – requires.

But for us, living and working today, to be trapped inside history like this seems a form of madness. With 'that one talent which is death to hide / Lodged with [us] useless', the fact that our granddaughters might – if we fight hard enough – be allowed to develop their full human and intellectual capacities is not quite consolation enough.

The problem's two-fold. We look at the canonised past and are not surprised that in the seventeenth, eighteenth and even nineteenth centuries, when most women were denied even rudimentary literacy, and were certainly shut out from the in-depth literary formation that a Classical education provided, they were creatively pre-eminent only in vernacular, anonymous genres. But wait a minute: this was historically true of most men, too, above all in colonised Ireland. Yet, since the Second World War, the sons of small farmers (Seamus Heaney) or village publicans (Brendan Kennelly) have had little problem breaking that pattern, both in their own work and, as a consequence, retrospectively. That's where the double fold comes in. As Anne Enright so brilliantly pointed out recently in the *London Review of Books*, we all – both men and women – read women more harshly than men. Even in 2018, it turns out, a male name is all it takes to assure us of an author's greater intentionality, seriousness, and hinterland of technical ability.

What goes for poets goes, to some extent, for critics too. Gender, as Lord Byron nearly said, 'Is of man's life a thing apart, / 'Tis woman's whole existence.' I'd like to think I've been invited to review *The Cambridge Companion to Irish Poets* because of my work as a senior poet-critic and editor (and because of the critical distance being British allows here). But the call from *PIR* comes but rarely, and I'm aware that I've probably been asked more simply because I'm a woman, and because this collection of essays has come under sustained fire for the relatively few women it canonises. Just to remind you of the figures: four of the thirty poets included are women, and four of the book's thirty contributors (thirty-one, including its editor) are female.

Walking into any such controversy is scary. The poetry world can be as intemperate and capable of groupthink as any pro-Trump rally. So let's start on a positive note. In one of the most substantial volumes to appear so far in the Cambridge Companion series, Gerald Dawe has assembled some of the best literary critical minds on the island of Ireland (and some who are based in the UK) to write about thirty key Irish poets. The result, considered chapter by chapter, is a cabinet of sophisticated delights. Scholar and poet as he is himself, Dawe has made the crucial decision to place Irish verse in the historical and political context which has formed it. A chronology of historical and literary/cultural events prefaces the book, which opens with Edmund Spenser in a salutary nod to the colonising context of the Elizabethan age. The balance between political career and poetry is summarised by Spenserian specialist Seán Lysaght with a deftness that sets the tone for the rest of the volume.

It also, of course, sets the tone for the volume's contents. These are, in their way, wide-ranging. Spenser is followed by Swift, Goldsmith, Moore, and Mangan before the volume even gets to Yeats. Also among these early chapters, Aodán Mac Póilin's essay on Aogán Ó'Raithille (c.1670–1729) is a scholarly reclamation of the early eighteenth-century Gaelic poet, who was 'a master of the techniques of Gaelic accentual verse', though unpublished in his lifetime. That this reclamation includes a reassessment of the subsequent English-language translations through which he's best known only reveals the complexity of the task Dawe has set himself.

Ireland has, famously, one of the richest poetry traditions in the world: but the challenge this sets is that there is in fact more than one Irish poetry tradition. There are the two languages: the *Companion* also includes Gaelic poets Seán Ó Ríordáin, Nuala Ní Dhomhnaill and, for one part of a complex creative life that Peter Sirr carefully outlines, Michael Hartnett. There are writers whose poetic development is explicitly involved with a developing Irish identity, whether personal or public cultural – in this book, the comfortable majority – and there are those, like Samuel Beckett, who leave, and become associated with European modernism. Then there are the various geopolitical and religious answers to the question of what Irish identity can be. Guy Woodward shows us the Methodist Ulsterman John Hewitt's use of landscape as a touchstone in his struggle to continue to belong to the island of Ireland after what Woodward accurately calls 'the partition' of 1921. Eavan Boland – who appears in this book, considered by Justin Quinn – has herself used the essay form as well as poetry to distil her project of defining Irish history as something created not simply in the public, masculine realm, but in women's domestic lives. In short, there are several traditions recorded here and it's perhaps little surprise that each has relatively few representatives.

Nevertheless, the question about why so few women have been included demands an answer, in part precisely because of this book's strengths. In dealing with *Irish* writing, and above all with *poets* rather than poems, the *Companion* is peculiarly and necessarily concerned with identity: absolutely the heading under which gender must be considered. Moreover the quality of the work that Dawe has elicited from his contributors means that this could otherwise be a go-to volume for years to come. And there's no point in playing a game of substitutions: every one of the poets included here is indispensable. Equally indispensable is the way this collection of essays builds a portrait of the interconnectedness of a culture as it is being made. Gifted but relatively unknown poets of any gender, scribbling at the dining table or riffing as they work in the yard, are beside its point.

This is, in fact, the deep-level theme literary scholars would do well to address. Boland has shown us how women's history is always *history*. We have mostly got as far reading overlooked women writers as responding to their own cultural times, and we reject the idea that they are simply feelingful näifs. But literary history, like history in general, is a story of successful influence. Women writers have often primarily influenced other women (fellow writers perhaps, but mostly their readers, or even simply correspondents), and have sometimes done so in informal, undervalued structures that have more in common with other vernacular forms now retrieved by historians of ideas, such as hedge schools or itinerant preaching, than with metropolitan literary-critical elites. To map these networks of influence would be to make an additional new case for the significance of our literary foremothers.

But what is an editor like Dawe to do meanwhile? It's a question, as the *Fired! Irish Women Poets and the Canon* pledge puts it, of good faith. Received opinion won't change unless we change it. A *Companion* to *poets* is necessarily a history of celebrated individuals; and celebrated individuals, historically, have largely been white men. No poets of colour appear in this volume. A wiser publisher than Cambridge University Press might have called this a *Companion to the History of Irish Poets*, thus drawing attention to the process of canon building in which it, like its precedents, is engaged. (Editing a contemporary periodical, as I found at *Poetry Review*, is far easier because there's just so much good work by women poets that keeping contributor figures balanced is easy.)

Though most remain at the height of their writing powers, none of the living poets the *Companion* includes is under sixty-five. The many possible good reasons for this include a need to see past reputational bubbles to a substantial body of work. But it would have been intelligent to break with the usual CUP formula and end this collection with a contextual essay addressing today's greater diversity. This could at least have identified the work of key middle-generation figures who have accumulated major bodies of work: a lengthy, varied list bound to include, for example, Rita Ann Higgins, Paula Meehan, Sinéad Morrissey. Better still would have been, either there or in the Introduction, to acknowledge that problems of representation are being posed here, since even women who have historically been canonised are strikingly absent. I was astonished to find no Mary Tighe, no Gore-Booth or Lady Gregory, and no Katharine Tynan.

It's a great deal more scholarly to acknowledge a problem or limit than to brush it under the carpet. But best of all, of course, would have been to include many more poets, all of them women, even if that meant shortening every chapter a little. What splendours we could then enjoy!

Fired! Irish Women Poets and the Canon

PREAMBLE TO THE PLEDGE

This is the preamble to a pledge aimed at redressing the gender imbalance in Irish poetry. The pledge, which we invite scholars and writers of all genders to sign, commits signatories to asking questions about gender representation.

Since the penning of this pledge was prompted by the announcement of *The Cambridge Companion to Irish Poets*, edited by Gerald Dawe (Cambridge University Press, 2017), we include here a brief account of the misrepresentation of women's contribution in Irish poetry in critical volumes like the *Cambridge Companion* as well as in anthologies, conferences, and other publications and events. We see the *Cambridge Companion* as a single stark iteration of a much wider problem.

We suggest some of the ways in which this volume might have acknowledged the contribution of women to Irish poetry. By drawing attention to women's contribution, we intend to set a positive example for future editors, publishers, teachers, and organizers in Irish literature.

Critical volumes such as *The Cambridge Companion to Irish Poets* are presented as surveys of the canon of our national literature, yet they frequently misrepresent our literature by failing to take account of the work of women writers. The absence of women poets from this and other publications leads to a distorted impression of our national literature and to a simplification of women's roles within it. The implication is that women are a minority in Irish poetry and literary criticism. They are not. In fact, it would not have been burdensome for the *Cambridge Companion* to more truthfully represent the gender balance in Irish poetry, since women's contribution to Irish poetry and Irish literary criticism is plentiful and rich. We find it difficult to comprehend that the gender imbalance of this volume was not questioned at any stage of the peer review process.

The Cambridge Companion to Irish Poets repeats the minimization or obliteration of women's poetry by previous anthologies and surveys. The most famous of these is the three-volume *Field Day Anthology of Irish Writing* (Field Day, 1991), but the process of exclusion pre-dates the Field Day project (Ní Dhomhnaill, 2002, and Keating, 2017). The *Companion* is part of a larger process by which the significance of works by women is attenuated as they become inaccessible or obscured, simply by virtue of their absence from canonical text books.

No women poets from the 18th, 19th and earlier 20th century are included in the forthcoming *Cambridge Companion*. Among the poets of the 18th century who might have been included are Laetitia Pilkington, Mary Barber, Mary Tighe, and Dorothea Herbert, while Charlotte Brooke's creative translation, *Reliques of Irish Poetry*, is unquestionably influential (Ní Mhunghaile, 2009). The influence of the 19th-century poet and novelist Emily Lawless on 20th-century Irish writers, to take another example, is repeatedly asserted in scholarship (Calahan, 1991, and Hansson, 2007). The *Cambridge Companion* does not take advantage of the work done on Irish women poets in the early Romantic period (Wright, 2006, and Behrendt, 2010). It does not take advantage of the work done on women's participation in the archipelagic coterie poetics at the time of Anne Southwell and Katherine Phillips (Prescott, 2014, Carpenter and Collins, 2014.) Nor does it attend to the poets of the Irish literary revival and the First World War, who include Katharine Tynan, Susan L Mitchell, Dora Sigerson Shorter, Ethna Carbery, Eva Gore-Booth, and Nora Hopper Chesson. The anthology *Voices on the Wind: Women Poets of the Celtic Twilight* has made work by these poets widely available and has argued for the centrality of women's writing to the Irish literary revival, when considered in its European context (Ní Dhuibhne, 1995).

In a volume that includes less well-established male poets from the mid-century, the absence of mid-century women poets is particularly striking. It is not new. The repeated neglect of these mid-century women poets in constructions of Irish literary history has been addressed by Fogarty (1999), Clutterbuck (1999), Schreibman (2001), Sullivan (2003), Collins (2012), and Mulhall (2012). The critical anthology *Poetry by Women in Ireland 1870-1970* has made the work of women poets from the mid-century widely available (Collins, 2012). Despite this availability, the powerfully subversive poetry of mid-century women poets is completely omitted from *The Cambridge Companion to Irish Poets*.

The Cambridge Companion misses an opportunity to introduce students and other readers to modernist, avant-garde, and experimental Irish poetry. Poets such as Lola Ridge, Freda Laughton, Blanaid Salkeld, Rhoda Coghill, Sheila Wingfield, Catherine Walsh, Máighréad Medbh, and Mairéad Byrne are poorly represented as it is, since there are few anthologies which highlight modernist and avant-garde Irish poetry. To redress this neglect, the current volume could have taken advantage of, for instance, Susan Schreibman's work on the poets of 1929-1959 (2001); work done by Daniel Tobin and Terese Svoboda on Lola Ridge (2004, 2016); Anne Fogarty's work on Rhoda Coghill (1999); Emma Penney's work on Freda Laughton (forthcoming); Alex Davis' work on Sheila Wingfield

(2001); Claire Bracken's work on Catherine Walsh (2005, 2008, 2016); Lucy Collins' work on Catherine Walsh (2015); and Moynagh Sullivan's work on Blanaid Selkeld (2003).

Failure to pay adequate attention to Irish-language poetry compounds the exclusion of women from *The Cambridge Companion to Irish Poets*, since it mitigates against the inclusion of, for instance, Máire Mhac an tSaoi, Caitlín Maude, Biddy Jenkinson, Éilís Ní Dhuibhne, Celia de Fréine, and Collette Ní Ghallchóir, as well as 18th-century oral women's poetry. There is significant scholarship to be drawn on, particularly in the case of Máire Mhac an tSaoi (Ed. De Paor, 2014, De Paor, 2013, Titley, 2012). The volume risks forfeiting the opportunity for a new generation of students and scholars to interrogate the place women poets writing in the Irish language have occupied in our national cultural development.

Finally, we note the absence of working-class women's poetry from volumes such as this. While little enough scholarship has been produced in this area, we might point for an obvious example to the work of Paula Meehan, who has engaged explicitly with the landscape and history of working-class Dublin in her poetry. We call on scholars, editors and publishers to attend to diversity in Irish poetry, in all its dimensions.

The absence of women from our critical volumes, literary surveys, and anthologies alters literary history and distorts the way we read contemporary women's poetry, raising a question for readers as to whether Irish women writers existed or exist today in any number. What message do we want to send to our young scholars? Will their contribution to Irish literature or literary criticism be deemed less valuable because they are women?

Notes

This essay was written collaboratively by 'Fired! Women Poets and the Canon', and originally published on Chris Murray's website at https://poethead.wordpress.com/2017/12/16/fired-irish-women-poets-and-the-canon-preamble-to-the-pledge/ 'Fired! Women Poets and the Canon' represents a convergence of practising women poets and academics from both the north and south of Ireland, who felt a response to the gender imbalance in *The Cambridge Companion to Irish Poets* (2017) was necessary.

For full acknowledgements, see
https://awomanpoetspledge.com/responses-to-fired/fired-acknowledgements/

To sign the pledge, go to https://awomanpoetspledge.com/

Ita O'Donovan

MAKING ROOM

I'm thinking of the curlew,
that we Irish call the hump-backed,
or *An Crotach*.
They look for open land that's damp,
not much to ask for in this country
yet they are not breeding here.
An adagio being lost
from the soundscape of our countryside.

The curlew has been around a long time,
appears on old Greek monuments
being given the genus name of *Numenius*,
or New Moon, sickle-shaped like his beak.
When I look at it, this scimitar
curving down his breast,
I wonder how he carries it,
until I note his knees,
back-to-front for balance.

I never see a flock of curlews
on the rocks below my house,
only one, possibly an immigrant,
announcing himself with his burbling triple cry,
always on a day that's damp,
or about to be, never luminous.
He has become my familiar; after sunny days
I'm watching out for grey, for moisture,
and that heart-aching cry.

Doireann Ní Ghríofa

AT DERRYNANE, I THINK OF EIBHLÍN DUBH AGAIN

In April, when the bog myrtle
begins to flicker in the thickets,

when crimson stems thicken with
the beginnings of catkins, they stretch

to a length that might tickle
a girl's knees, a girl who might be

running through bramble and bracken,
laughing over her shoulder, to a home

that waits steady in stone. Every time
I read your words *Mo chara is m'uan tú,*

I wonder where they buried you.
If I could find your gravestone,

I would bring you no rose, Eibhlín,
I would carry a fistful of myrtle stems

bound in twine, a small bundle
tied tight and neat to place at your feet.

David Sergeant

SONNET LOOKING, FOR SOPHIE

'Death becomes you.'

when you're so prised off that the dream-realm
which no-one believes in is speaking
in story and the structure at the helm
has read your work and is trying

to speak it back to you, but it
becomes the misread oracle of war
you know about but still
you block the light you would be seen

by by you, the pattern
acknowledged in your displacement
into pattern where you
can be and the truth

is a fiction, I mean, that is the truth.

Katie Donovan

NAMING THESE THINGS

Jean Bleakney, *Selected Poems* (Templar Poetry, 2016), £12.99.
Mark Granier, *Ghostlight: New and Selected Poems* (Salmon Poetry, 2017), €12.
Mary Dorcey, *To Air the Soul, Throw All the Windows Wide: New and Selected Poems* (Salmon Poetry, 2016), €12.

'Naming these things is the love-act and its pledge; / For we must record love's mystery without claptrap' – lines from Patrick Kavanagh's poem 'The Hospital' come to mind when perusing these three new volumes of *Selected Poems*.

With titles such as 'The Valentine Rose' and 'Blue Hydrangeas', Jean Bleakney's passion for plants is clear: gardens, the labour of the gardener, and the exact science of the botanist are central concerns in her work. Led by her wry, enquiring voice, the reader is shepherded on unpredictable journeys, far from the well-trodden terrain of Plath's tulips or Wordsworth's daffodils. In 'Mock Orange', written for 12th July 1998, the 'rescinded petals' resemble 'piecemeal shrouds'.

Not for Bleakney the 'fug' of poets from Kavanagh to Sappho, who appropriate plants to serve their muse without getting their facts right: 'Were you having a go, Paddy? ... / Was memory shook? Was the book poorly illustrated? / Or was it viewed in the dim imperative of a Dublin snug?' (from 'Imitation', subtitled *On looking into Patrick Kavanagh's "On Reading a Book on Common Wild Flowers"*').

Bleakney's *Selected Poems* includes at least two-thirds of the contents of her first three collections: *The Ripple Tank Experiment* (1999); *The Poet's Ivy* (2003); and *ions* (2011), all published by Lagan Press. The cover is a gorgeous front to back reproduction of a pastoral scene by the Hungarian artist Tivadar Csontváry Kosztka. With its 'arboretum of blue-greens', the painting is the subject of the poem 'Csontváry's Flowers', where Bleakney investigates the artist's visionary but intriguingly odd-angled process of composition.

As itemised in her poem 'Looking Up', Bleakney's diverse subjects include 'the weird, the lovely and the risqué', with the appeal of language and its potential a spur. Some of the weaker poems are slight, overly chatty and weighed down with parentheses. But these are minor cavils.

Bleakney's restless intelligence ranges from science to farm ritual and dialect. Newry-born and Belfast-based, Bleakney was shipped off to spend summer holidays with her farming relatives. Vivid memories of this displacement – a theme she shares with her near contemporary, the Dublin-based poet Siobhán Campbell – are colourfully expressed in one of her finest poems, 'Evocation':

Half-repulsed, half-scared of hen house, dairy, byre
and penned bull, ready and waiting to sire;
and the flies from the 'duckle' of cowshit
and the twin-holed plank of the outside toilet;
and the grin … the rotten teeth of Tommy Ovens
as he cycled past.

With regard to structure, Bleakney's end rhymes are neatly and fluently achieved, and in *ions* she encapsulates the collection as an orderly series of alphabetical meditations. However, part of the appeal of her work is her witty resignation in the face of the physical world's 'ping-along thing-ness', which refuses neat categories and is always ready to surprise her – even, as in 'Self Portraits with Measuring Tape', by the dimensions of her own body. 'The Physics of a Marriage' includes the wonderful image of 'the ripple tank experiment' from whence came the title of her first collection: 'even though the floor got soaked / the pattern somehow held'.

In 'Acceleration', the poem takes off, in typical Bleakney fashion, with a lovely blend of assonance; references to science; and droll asides. In spite of her rueful comparison of her addled brain to that of Hopkins – hers, riddled with 'potholes'; his, more dramatically, riven by 'cliffs of fall' – the poem ends as an irresistible celebration of the whimsical associations of that flawed brain's consciousness: 'setting … a word and its inscape twanging'.

While Bleakney has a professional life as a gardener, Mark Granier is a photographer of some renown. This heightened artistic awareness gives his poetry its own visual stamp, and includes nods to Jack Yeats, Picasso, Rembrandt, and Van Gogh. The cumulative effect is that of a series of snapshots, often Dublin-based. Places are named – Ringsend, St Stephen's Green, Grafton Street, Fade Street – and atmospheres evoked: 'coughing, whiskey-lit, smoke-signalled city; its fug / louring in low clouds'.

Laced with references to light and landscape, *Ghostlight: New and Selected Poems* contains 20 new poems along with work from Granier's first four collections. *Airborne* (Salmon Poetry), his first book, appeared in 2001, and was followed by *The Sky Road* (Salmon Poetry, 2007); *Fade Street* (Salt Publishing, 2010); and *Haunt* (Salmon Poetry, 2015). The poet Liam Ó Muirthile provides a thoughtful introduction to this *Selected Poems*.

In poems such as 'Find' and 'Bullseye', Granier captures the essence of objects and sounds: 'rooks, their cries / sharp as springs bursting from the sky's mattress'. This can sometimes feel list-like, lacking an end point. More memorably, poems like 'Seascape in Clare' and 'Grip Stick' conclude with bold and suggestive imagery: 'We ordered oysters [...] each one a nacreous bloom, a cool bed / peeled back to the sheets'. Granier is at pains to remind us that his natural stance is that of observer – of himself in his various guises, and of the world around him, whether it be a cityscape or a kitchen. There is much to enjoy when the reader settles down to share his tender, finely-crafted observations: 'this / mammal-mark, shared scar / / remembers' (from 'Navels'). Like Bleakney's, his self-deprecating, informed, and subtle voice is highly appealing, especially when it is let off the leash to play.

At a deeper level – and suggested by Granier's titles – the work circles back to a sense of absence, which the poet attempts to fill with what he can name in the world. Who am I, where do I fit in, and where have I come from? These are the big questions that keep writers on the job, and in Granier's oeuvre, they are mooted without any obvious resolution, as in '7Up, Torremolinos' : 'The universe is utterly / beyond me, but close. Close.'

In a new poem, 'Tube', Granier refers to a youth spent between the cities of London and Dublin, before going on to capture, with uncanny precision, the exact scent of the London Underground: 'brushed by that warm / intimate-exotic wind – smells of caked soot, / historical dust'. Here, typically, Granier hovers on the sidelines of memory, in a vacuum where everyone else is on the move.

Similarly, in the title poem of *Haunt*, he dreams of his grandfather in his childhood home which has already been sold. In 'Fruit Machine' – one of the finest poems in the book, about the vagaries of fate – the poet skids on black ice and narrowly misses crashing: 'lemons, cherries, black bars, a trance, a trip / through a hole in the world'.

In another fine poem, 'From Blackrock', Granier cites not knowing his father as the cause of his 'soft spot for absences'. But in Granier's best poems, his affinity with absence lingers as an eloquent expression of the uncertainties of our increasingly unmoored contemporary existence.

Mary Dorcey's *To Air the Soul, Throw All the Windows Wide* features 34 new poems as well as work from five earlier collections – *Kindling* (Onlywomen Press, 1982); *Moving into the Space Cleared by Our Mothers* (Salmon Poetry, 1991); *The River that Carries Me* (Salmon Poetry, 1995); *Like Joy in Season, Like Sorrow* (Salmon Poetry, 2001); and *Perhaps the Heart is Constant After All* (Salmon Poetry, 2012).

Dorcey is a poet who celebrates relationships between women – whether lovers, or mothers and daughters. Her strength lies in naming the ever-shifting nuances of these intimate bonds. She broke new ground when her celebratory poems about the erotic love between women were first published in the 1980s, at a time when this was, as the euphemism goes, 'neither fashionable nor profitable'.

The love poetry is written from the perspective of the one who watches and savours the physical beauties of her partner, whether in the heat of flirtation and desire, or in the melancholy aftermath of loss. There are also lyrical evocations of places where love has been shared: 'a beach at evening, / the gorse in full bloom / the sky livid' ('Teach Me to Remember'). Written with assurance and spontaneity, the poem 'Taking

Shelter' hinges on a shared umbrella, where the loved one ties up her hair: 'the innocent provocation / of your ear'.

Dorcey's style begins simply, conversationally, and builds up force with a litany of persuasive, sometimes humorous, repetitions. However powerfully this may come across in the context of a live performance, on the page this style risks rendering some of the poems slack and predictable. 'The Ordinary Woman' which spans three pages, is a case in point.

Yet Dorcey's endings have impact, satisfying the reader with an eloquent, arresting image: 'As if death were a foolish, / extravagant hat you were trying on for size' (from 'Trying on for Size'); or 'Who made you a blade / I cannot dare to handle?' (from 'I Cannot Love You as You Want to Be Loved').

Set in that most romantic of locations, a railway station, one of her finest love poems is 'Return' (from *Moving into the Spaces Cleared by Our Mothers*). Reminiscent of John Montague's classic 'All Legendary Obstacles' (1965), Dorcey anticipates re-uniting with her lover: 'The sky / will shift as I step out, a handful / Of sun thrust down on your hair.' While Montague's poem feels like a scene from a black and white movie, Dorcey's is bouncing with colour.

Dorcey's style can be marred by awkward line breaks, but she is fluent with rhyme, particularly in the early work. In more recent poems, her stanzas can seem rather like paragraphs. A new poem which is written in this latter style but retains occasional rhymes is 'An Argument with Fate'. Here death is personified – refreshingly – as a 'voracious old slut' whom the living enslave themselves to placate.

Dorcey's latest work is infused with a sense of mortality and the book ends with a powerful rendition of her mother's death. With 'Parting', she abandons the lyric mode for a more contemporary hybrid of prose and verse: 'what / was most hard to endure we found a way to make bearable. And / this famous scene, this dying now, was only one more thing / we had to get right between us.'

Three poets and their acts of naming are represented here, in three very different volumes, but each, in the words of Kavanagh, manages to 'Snatch out of time the passionate transitory'. New poems by Granier and Dorcey reassure us that more work is on the way, and Jean Bleakney has already launched a fourth full collection, *No Remedy*, from Templar Poetry.

Stiofán Ó hIfearnáin

AN MHÁTHAIR ADHMAID AGUS A MAC

I.

Chailleamar í ar a haistear aerga,
Idir coill an aitil agus sceach an aitinn:
Áit bhaolach í an teorainn.

Thit sí an nóiméad a cheap sí
Go raibh an deighilt slán aici.

... i nduilliúir na coille
a chodlaíonn a hanam ...

Maidir leis an gcorp
Tá sé fós linne.

Na soilse múchta
i gcipíní na súile.

II.

Milltí aríst is aríst é:
Go dtí gur dhein sé dearmhad
Cé go díreach a bhí ann –

Créatúir
A shiúileadh na sráideanna:
gan mheas. Gan moladh ó éinne.

Chonac ar maidin
In éadaí na cille é:
An tsochraid réamh-ullmhaithe aige.

Níl eadrainn ach an chónra.

Stiofán Ó hIfearnáin

THE WOODMOTHER AND HER SON

WOODMOTHER

She slipped our grasp on an airy path
between juniper wood and thorny gorse,
a perilous spot on the frontier.

Almost clear of the faery door,
she stumbled into Otherwhere.

Among fallen leaves
her spirit sleeps.

Though we've led her home,
she's numb as seasoned elm,

no spark kindles
her ashen eyes.

THE WOODMOTHER'S SON

Hard words whittled him
till he forgot his own grain,

miserable creature,
a go-the-road
without worth or standing.

This morning I saw him
dressed in his Sunday best
for his pre-planned burial.

The coffin's gleam
reflects our sameness.

– translation by **Breda Wall Ryan** of 'An mháthair adhmaid agus a mac'

Leah Keane

THE AULD FELLA'S PRE-BIRTHDAY DINNER

It started with a call at one in the afternoon
during the rugby (Ireland v Scotland)
on a Saturday (three days before his birthday).
It's never good when he calls this early.

Stoic red letters warn of an incoming.
Still, I answer the phone.
Immediately I know
from his shaky joviality
that later we'll be having a dinner
full of teeth grinding.

I've always marvelled at his ability
to say the same things differently.
There are only so many ways
I can say I'm fine
before it becomes untrue.

I eventually hang up
with an exasperated *see you later.*
I look to my brother on the couch
(he'd come back from London especially).

What did he want? he asks.
I don't know.
Scotland score a try.
But it sounds like he's had a few.

His chest rises quickly then retreats.
A click of the tongue, shake of the head.
Pure disgust.

*The one fuckin' day I ask him to stay out of the pub
and he can't even do that for me.*
He goes outside for a cigarette.

We pick him up at five. He sits in the front with Dan.
I'm directly behind him, Aaron's beside me.
We're a few minutes out the road when he enquires

Where's her ladyship this evening?
Who? Dan asks.
Leah.

My brother shakes his head. He's got that look from before.
She's sitting right behind you, ya prick
and continues driving.
The Auld Fella laughs
and reaches a hand behind in greeting.
I recoil so sharply it shocks me.

At the restaurant he analyses a painting of four cows.
It's in black and white but he can still make out
they're Hereford Crosses with Angus heads on them.
The middle one was dehorned at an early age.
Another had slipped a calf.
It's grand for a while.

He orders a 228 steak. The most expensive thing on the menu.
Takes one bite then looks at the floor.
He can't eat it because he had something earlier.
Couldn't you have just waited a few hours? I ask.
He could, but that's an unfair verb.

His chest jumps. It looks as though he might throw up
but I can't find sympathy for him in this moment.

We drive him home.
He asks if we'd like to stay for a while.
None of us do.

Dan O'Brien

ONE HUNDRED AND THREE

Sundays
In Ireland
All that fall

I'd walk
Because Jesus
What else

Can one do
When life locks
Itself into

A stone
Statue of
Michael Collins

Hidden amid
The alien
Moss

The old world
Roaring delicious
Behind shutters

The same panic
Walks with me
Lately

The wind
Educated the ivy
In the quadrangle

As I lingered
Another day
Into night

Briege Duffaud

WASTELAND

Every year in bleak bored winter the Dublin actors came
to towns across the North. Anew McMaster and his touring plays,
Pinter's old troupe: too young we missed him by five years.
Anew played Hamlet, Lear, the Scottish king, in Town Halls hushed

with awe-held breath of shop-boys, clerks and farmers' wives,
front rows rich with scented privilege. Convent boarders gaped
at tall Lord Wakehurst and his wife, cousins of the Queen.
A traitor curtsied in my star-struck head dreaming of courtly love.

For weeks Ophelia, robed in satin quilt, drowned on the
dormitory floor, Polonius groaned his last behind thick linen curtains.
Lady Macbeth scrubbed away, Camay soap and nailbrush.
Faces of the Dublin actors displaced young priests in teenage fantasies.

I Google them and read old memories much like mine:
teachers, writers, politicians: our small provincial lives
illumined by those Winters' tales played to a silenced hall of
mingled Taigs and Prods united in delight one week a year.

And you? I ask my English friend, *did you play Portia in your Surrey dorm?*
Clash swords by torchlight while Matron slept? She laughs: *Christ no! we*
swooned over Elvis, kissed photos of Mick, sneaked out the windows to Eel Pie Island.
So sad, you lot, reared in a wasteland. No wonder you rebelled in the end
and took to killing each other. We lived in the real world, says she. Unsmiling.

Andy Eaton

ON COLLAPSE

I should have heard the man and grown familiar
with the scent of his shirt after work,
the look of those hands, the pencil lead rubbed in

the finger grain, the earth black crescents under his nails.
He lifted cars from off his chest, they say,
sent my father to the fusebox

while he shook there on the metal folding chair
– voltage where blood should be –
to finish wiring the hall light.

They say he knocked a bull
out cold, where it began to charge
my infant aunt. Tipping back

from his hand, one punch,
the bull fell like a cabinet off a truck bed.

Thomas McCarthy

THE SADDEST MUSIC

Dennis O'Driscoll, *Collected Poems* (Carcanet Press, 2017), £19.99.

Where to begin with Dennis O'Driscoll? His untimely death in 2012 was tragic, not just for his beloved family, but for hundreds of readers and followers of poetry. His was a prodigious talent, witty, ironic, sardonic, prophetic, but his influence as commentator, editor, and general 'cheerer-upper' of the entire Irish poetic scene was priceless and irreplaceable. He was on first-name terms with scores of writers across the world. He had read the works of hundreds of poets thoroughly and he had formed a very settled and definite opinion on their value as artists. He shared these opinions in published commentary and edited editions, as well as upon hastily scribbled postcards and lengthy early evening phone-calls. A collection of his urgently scribbled yet elegant postcards would probably form his best biography. An Irish poet might be published in the most obscure small journal, but Dennis would unearth the work and make a comment. A goodly portion of this bustling energy and commentary is captured in *Troubled Thoughts, Majestic Dreams* and *The Outnumbered Poet*, his two prose books published by The Gallery Press. A senior public servant like CH Sisson or Archibald MacLeish, O'Driscoll adored the world created by poets and poetry. He trusted this world and all its reversals and reverberations: he would have had no other world. He published nine collections of well-crafted and fully premeditated poetry. His last collection, *Update*, published posthumously in 2014 and a PBS Special Commendation, was also the swan song of Peter Jay's Anvil Press Poetry in London. O'Driscoll's posthumous future now lies with that great Manchester mothership of poetry, Carcanet Press, and with Copper Canyon Press in the United States. Yes, he was a distinctly Irish poet, that need hardly be said, but his world contained Michael Hamburger and Miroslav Holub – he was as involved in their tones and biographies as if they were also from a busy town in Co Tipperary.

The first time I heard Dennis O'Driscoll's name mentioned, it was mentioned with alarm. The voice calling his name on the stairs of 6, Sidney Place, Cork, was that of the young Waterford poet, Seán Dunne:

> "Shit, McCarthy, did you know that Dennis O'Driscoll is a Munster-man?"
> "He's not," I explained, "doesn't he write for *Hibernia* and isn't he a civil servant in Dublin? He's a Dubliner."
> "No, he's not. He's from Tipperary and he's just written to me. His poems are amazing. He should be in my anthology."

That was more than thirty years ago when Seán was editing his *Poets of Munster*, the first such anthology since O'Daly's *The Poets and Poetry of Munster* in 1849. What worried the young Waterford editor was that the ink was nearly dry on his selection and he held in his hand a sheaf of a Tipperary man's work that couldn't be omitted because it was so good. Swift revisions were made and poems were shunted overboard to make space for poems like this:

AFTER VINOKUROV

Objects speak louder than words.

And here is the stone that made the river dance.
Here is the gate that opened to friends once.

'Being', a poem for Julie O'Callaghan, would contain sections titled 'Entropy,' 'Skeleton,' and 'Death' – which contained the lines 'what will be our certified cause of death / will we expire with the lost memory of arteriosclerosis / dissolving in alcohol, crumbling with pain / basted in our own body fat, shivering with old age'. He was still in his twenties when he wrote those lines.

That was in the early 1980s: the poet of *Kist* from Dolmen Press had been located correctly, and a distinctive voice in Irish poetry had announced itself. Such flinty darkness in a poet so young was both impressive and strangely attractive. "What'll I say about a fella like this?" Seán continued, balancing on the dodgy stairs, "he must be dying or something. I'll have a chat with John Ennis about him." More than thirty years later, in *Update*, O'Driscoll would continue to provoke us in that tone he established so early:

And did his warriors not go on
to ask Fionn what the saddest music is?

I catch an old-style sing-song from
My Alzheimer neighbour's house.
                    – THE GOOD OLD DAYS

This *Collected Poems* is a magisterial book with an apt and haunting cover design from a painting by the equally enigmatic Martin Gale. It allows the prosecutor O'Driscoll to rest his case. He has collected all the Capital taxes owed to life and handed them over to that universal Revenue of posterity. The sustained tones are impressive, reassuring, shocking. We see his topical commentary, his would-be editorials written at the last minute to midnight. His sense of humour is dominant and persuasive, but we know from the biographies of many comedians how a compelling sense of humour can be a carefully basted crust above a deeper darkness:

> Out of the dung heap of chemical spills,
> a thornless mutant rose will sprout,
> its scent as fragrant as a new deodorant spray.
> — LOOKING FORWARD

Like Theodore Roethke, he knew a thing or two about dung heaps, chemicals, and sprouts, coming, as he did, from the most successful rose-growing family in Munster; from the O'Driscoll Gardens of Thurles. A sensory darkness, a persistent habit of cataloguing and categorising, an understanding of processes of disease, decay, and rebirth in both plants and humans, all form part of the architecture of O'Driscoll's literary biography. In 'The Bottom Line' he writes: 'my brain is crammed with / transient knowledge', but what actually distinguishes his voice is the recurrent, persistent knowingness of his statements and confessions. His thoughts are rooted in insight and learning: it is this life that's transient. He got better, darker, funnier, as he went on. *Reality Check* (2007) and *Dear Life* (2012) are arguably his best books. In 'Skywriting' he could meditate in a complex weave like this:

> A laburnum resurgence sighted through a pergola.
> Unimpeded light – every pore translucent – recalling
> an age when the sun looked indulgently on a world
> in its prime, a planet slanted in favour of its rays
> yet unable to absorb so much illumination at one time.

In *Dear Life*, the urgency of life becomes more intense, the poet becomes impatient for knowledge and impatient to teach it:

> And spare us the dawn chorus
> that outwears its welcome
> like a loquacious breakfast guest.
>
> Spare us, therefore, the spring,
> its fake sincerity, its unethical
> marketing strategies, its deceptive
> pledges, its built-in obsolescence,
> its weeds breeding like flies.
> — SPARE US

Where did the poet find such a tone? In which part of Irish life did it become available to him? His was a humanist unhappiness, not an Irish Catholic one. The anxieties of an Austin Clarke, a John Montague, a Máirtín Ó Direáin, were irrelevant to him. His anxieties had a Scandinavian quality. His ironic good humour in the face of unknowing, in the face of a Christ-less truth, is European, it is Tranströmer-like. His poetic ancestors come from very far away, further East, maybe; from the heartland of what was the Slavic-grey land beyond the Berlin Wall. He invokes not Yeats, not AE, not some reconstructed Celtic myth-maker, but Zbigniew Herbert, Wisława Szymborska, and Miroslav Holub. He wanted to be as sardonic as Holub, as Berlin-sounding as Michael Hamburger, as decentralised and improvisational as George Szirtes. He wanted to be nowhere and therefore everywhere: in this he succeeded brilliantly. In this he had a courage not available to any other Irish poet. Even his memory of his own Thurles is 'after Zbigniew Herbert'. In book upon book he gave us an earful of this courage and, as if to drive his message home, he placed this epigraph from Paul Valéry at the beginning of the last collection he assembled, *Dear Life*: 'God made everything out of nothing, / but the nothingness shows through.' For all their pyrotechnics and radical beginnings, most Irish poets will eventually settle under the cultural-political umbrellas of either Patrick Kavanagh or John Hewitt, but O'Driscoll's imagination and aesthetic was radically, incorrigibly, unconventional to the end:

No one can look at death or the sun
without being left entirely in the dark.
Nor, with impunity, may the sun
expect to gaze directly at the moon.
Awestruck birds, fallen silent
before totality, know this when
the sun, corona blazing, is deposed.

The above words are, again, from 'Skywriting,' one of his finest poems. That Slavic despair, rescued by irony, is always there. Szymborska's 'The One Twenty Pub' and Holub's 'Experimental Animals', as well as the epigraph to O'Driscoll's own 'Crowd Scene' that is also taken from Szymborska, all act as signposts and cyphers to direct us away from Irish commentary; away from ourselves and the place where O'Driscoll might be judged too narrowly. His brain may have been crammed with transient knowledge, but he knew what he was doing as an artist. He never deviated from his determined projects. Even his great Heaney interview project, *Stepping Stones*, gives us a considered view of O'Driscoll as much as the view of Heaney – his obsessive, curious biopsy of the Nobel Laureate is really the most unguarded and valuable portrait of O'Driscoll at work. This *Collected Poems* also creates the last major portrait of the poet at his desk, in his office at Dublin Castle and working, thinking, obsessing, late into the night in his study at home. Here is a poet of lists ('Everyday asthma and brain tumour. / Everyday chilblains, cancers, coronaries. / Everyday depression and epilepsy'), and a poet of sequences, like 'Residuary Estates', 'Churchyard View: The New Estate', and 'Dear Life' – a poet who tried many conventional poetic forms to control his riotous impulses of despair. His was a life of awesome poetic responsibility, lived fully and lived very, very well. He illuminated everything he touched and challenged everyone to try harder, to do better. This great *Collected* seems less like a monument to a poet and more like a huge compression chamber from which the reader may emerge rinsed of all Irishness, struggling for breath.

Özgecan Kesici

THE CONSEQUENCES OF SILENCE

She sent me a song
I did not touch.
It flew over my body like a
pigeon on North Earl Street.

              I had scars in my palms.
              Long nails in half-moons
              that marked the end of fasting.

And we ate.
The lambs and the vines,
the hummingbirds and
our sorrows.

              She draped gold around my neck,
              hung bangles up to my elbows.
              I shone for days.
              They grew heavy.
              No returns –

She said she'd leave over her dead body
after he bruised her eye
with a plastic bottle
and we inhaled our birds,
suffocated them in our throats.

              Silver is lighter.

There are children singing
in the streets outside her mind.

              She dropped a mothball shawl on my shoulders.
              I tried to forget her hopeful gaze.
              I swallowed my bird into my stomach
              and drowned its flutter –

She recalls only what hasn't happened.
The catastrophes
distract her.

              I crush sour raspberries in my mouth,
              open wide to shock red
              and a song.

Travis Mossotti

WINE FRIDGE

A wine fridge, used gently, free for pickup
on Craigslist; it rests there because, quite simply,
capitalism requires that such novelties accrue
when the middle class suffers a glut of bonus
income come February, and I don't know how
much cheap wine fits inside, but Kendall-Jackson
comes to mind as the only bulk white I recall
from the country club where I worked banquets
at sixteen so I could afford to #heymister beer
and gun it across the county line and disappear,
for what it was worth, into a bonfire where
I must've said at least a dozen times, *Fuck*
this penguin outfit or *Fuck those goddamned*
rich-ass motherfuckers or *Pass me a smoke,*
I got a light. Still, that wine fridge will never
cross my lawn, let alone front-door threshold,
the same way my sixteen-year-old self will
never give up chain smoking or believing
in the beautiful death or staring bewilderedly
out from inside my body's bones at what's left
of him that I've kept shelved in a plastic bin
on the unfinished side of the basement. A few
pictures and a journal. Maybe a soccer trophy?
His disappointment will just have to get in line
with the rest of me, because old age crushes
boutonnières into the shape of a wine fridge,
a fucking fridge designed for the purpose
of keeping wine at less than room temperature.
I hate wine. And yet here it is now, smack dab
in the middle of my poem, which is just what
I need. One more absurd, impossible thing
I have somehow been charged with getting rid of.

Tim Cunningham

THE ANCESTRAL PILE REVISITED

Six years young, hair combed,
Shoes polished, neatly parcelled
And posted from the station,
C.I.E.'s dactyl wheels delivered me,
Second class, to Newcastle West.
Collected then by Tom and plonked
On his cart for the bouncy castle ride
Down rutted boreens he mistook
For Rome's Circus Maximus,
All the way to my grandmother's cottage,
My father's home before 'the boat',
Bari's field hospital and the fresh war grave.

Delivered again this morning
In my friend's Renault Scenic,
No hair left to comb, we followed
The not-quite-straight Sat Nav arrow
Past brown-black bogland, the white
Knuckle roots of upturned trees
And the green lapping waves of ferns
To the familiar, familial name, the hidden
In time half acre of Ballyloughane.

The cottage maintained its mystery,
Refused to reappear from the mist
Like some mythic Brigadoon.
The stepping stones stayed hidden,
Stepping stones between then and now
Across the stream turned intimate Styx.

Years have strong fingers.
They stripped the golden thatch,
Stone by stone dismantled
The limewashed home,
Reduced it to rubble. But why
Can't rubble be a pyramid?

Buried there, the evocative turf smoke,
The border collie's bark, the croak

Of a frog spared from the scythe,
The smell of my grandmother's daily bread,
Her tearful smile at the half door
Watching me, the shadow of her son, at play.
And, of course, the full moon clock
Ghosting the kitchen wall,
Telling hour and minute but keeping
Its vow to the secrets of time.

The speckled choir of thrushes on the rocks
Was pure imagination.

Breda Spaight

EPIPHANY

Why weren't you more fuckin' careful?
Didn't you know it wasn't safe, like?
Are you sure? Like, maybe there's a mistake?
I mean, you're not getting younger, y'know.
Things change, don't they, like? A mistake.
I mean to say, there're things women can do.
Like, like . . . Another fuckin' mouth to feed!
Things. You know? Women can do.

It's hard for her to remember him young.
To remember any of them. All hot hands;
come with me. When he asked to walk her home,
she liked his green eyes. *He'll do.*

The radio was playing *Down by the Salley Gardens*,
and all the boys from her parish were taking the boat.

Laura Linares

DROP ANCHOR

Edited by Manuela Palacios, calligraphies by Hachemi Mokrane, *Migrant Shores: Irish, Moroccan and Galician Poetry* (Salmon Poetry, 2017), €12.

With *Migrant Shores: Irish, Moroccan and Galician Poetry*, Manuela Palacios continues her excellent record of collaborations with poets living in and across various communities related to the Atlantic. Examples such as *Forkcd Tongues: Galician, Basque and Catalan Women's Poetry in Translations by Irish Writers* (Shearsman Books, 2012), *To the Winds our Sails: Irish Writers Translate Galician Poetry* (Salmon Poetry, 2010, with Mary O'Donnell), *Los Ritos de los Sentidos* (CantArabia, 2015, with Jaouad Elouafi, Bahi Takkouche, and Arturo Casas Vales), and *Pluriversos: Seis poetas irlandesas de hoxe* (Follas Novas, 2003) stand as testament to her continued dedication to the promotion of these linguistic and cultural realities and the facilitation of fruitful interactions. This beautiful collection, elegantly brought to us by Salmon Poetry and featuring the stunning calligraphies of Hachemi Mokrane, includes, after a succinct but thought-provoking introduction by the editor, a collection of poems from seven Moroccan and seven Galician authors who have been translated and creatively responded to by fourteen of the most stimulating contemporary Irish poets. Through this dynamic exchange, Palacios aims to follow the paths and lives of migrants and exiles from various cultural and social backgrounds, to provide a vivid illustration of her claim, perhaps more relevant now than ever, that 'to exist is to move forward'. Defying traditional ideas of the nation-state and of political and geographical boundaries by exploring the idea of hybridity and bringing together a wide array of voices connected through their shores rather than their lands, Palacios hints at alternative connections built around the Atlantic, explicit in the waters linking the three countries represented in the book, as well as implicit through historical migration routes, particularly in Galicia and Ireland. 'The Sea is History', and this volume actively engages with the currents and countercurrents experienced by those often forgotten by the history books.

The anthology sets out to give priority to the intersection between gender and diaspora: many poems in the collection explore the burdens and longings of the migrant woman. Around this powerful central axis, the collection also explores creative responses to the current refugee crisis, the migrant's body in movement or otherwise, the relationship between diaspora and memory, the liminal spaces inhabited by 'outsiders', and the opportunities and violences of the transculturation brought about by crossings. Eminent poets Mohammed Bennis and Paula Meehan begin the collection with a reflection on exile, memory, and life's constant learning and unlearning. Constraints to femininity and female desire imposed by different cultures are explored by Taha Adnan and his tongue-twisted Maroxelloise, as well as by his paired poet in the collection, Máighréad Medbh, with her account of a young Irish woman rejected by her family. Fatima Zahra Bennis and Susan Connolly continue with the topic of female desire in two gripping poems which, reflecting each other's structure, take the reader from the longing of one woman to another one's anxiety. Aicha Bassry's distressed woman waiting to cross a border encounters a compassionate response in Sarah Clancy's expression of powerlessness when faced with the refugee crisis, which is also present in the poignant poems offered by Imane El Khattabi and Hugh O'Donnell, while Mohamed Ahmed Bennis and Catherine Phil MacCarthy present two exceptionally evocative explorations of notions of detachment, dislocation, and uprooting. Ending the Moroccan-Irish section, Mezouar El Idrissi invokes an optimistic night in Granada to celebrate multicultural life and love, slightly toned down by Thomas McCarthy who, nonetheless, explores the power of words to establish bridges and provide freedom, in an illustrative image of the successes of this volume.

In the Irish-Galician section, the intricacies of the female migrant's experience are present across most of the poems, starting with Martín Veiga and Eiléan Ní Chuilleanáin's engrossing stories of female transatlantic migrations. Chus Pato and Lorna Shaughnessy examine the role of photographs to convey the absence from, and the difficulty of communication with, those left behind, while Marilar Aleixandre imagines a lunar escape to the exploitation suffered by African women. Her images of long journeys on foot are taken up by Breda Wall Ryan to illustrate the forced pilgrimage of today's refugees. Eva Veiga offers a compelling image of the urge to escape from an unrecognizable self, responded to by Maurice Harmon who, in line with Imane El Khattabi and Hugh O'Donnell, focuses on the refugee crisis, highlighting the West's blinding amnesia about our own migrating past. Baldo Ramos tells the story of his migrant family in the United States by linking their own tale to that of a transplanted tree, and is followed by Celia de Fréine who, in her response, interweaves Irish history of migration to the West Coast of the United States with the current refugee experience. Gonzalo Hermo rebels against normative impositions with potent imagery, echoed in Keith Payne's response, in which he explores the female outsider's invisibility, which is also examined in the last two poems of the collection, by María do Cebreiro and Mary O'Donnell, who focus on the entrapment suffered by women in the red light districts of Barcelona and Amsterdam.

Through an impeccable choice of pairings, Palacios facilitates stimulating dialogue between the poets who, besides, also seem to have found many other areas of common ground and connections that the reader will be able to discover as she navigates through the pages. Highlighting Bassry's and Payne's effective use of the image of the window, or the shared anger and hopelessness in Medbh, El Khattabi, O'Donnell, and Harmon's poems on the refugee crisis only scratches the surface of the many possibilities offered by this volume of poems, in constant conversation with each other. These exchanges are made possible by the translations provided by the Irish poets, mostly with the help of English drafts and the editor's linguistic support. In a brief response to the eternal debate as to whether poetry is better conveyed in other languages by translators or by poets, Palacios argues for the poets' ability to provide more refined creative renderings. I would, for my part, argue that this book is strong evidence of the futility of strict categorisation: there is no doubt that the authors' poetic sensitivity and experience is of utmost importance to convey their counterparts' poems, yet their attentiveness to cultural difference and their openness to inquiry and exploration leave no doubt that they can *also* be defined as translators. What is certain is that the constant interaction between the participants and the editor, coupled with the precision and rigour in their work, are clearly successful in this collection, in which the quality of the versions is undeniable. If Michael Cronin had described Palacios' and O'Donnell's previous volume, *To the Winds our Sails,* as one in which translation was clearly showcased as the 'supreme art of discovery', *Migrant Shores* eloquently illustrates translation as the art of deep listening and purposeful conversation, of acknowledgment of the Other and co-construction of new shared horizons.

Migrant Shores is not only a beautiful book both in content and in form, but also a necessary one. At a time in which pressing issues relating to political, economic, and ecological displacements have a central space in our day-to-day lives, as does our increased difficulty to listen deeply and maintain meaningful dialogue in public life, this book offers a window into a world of fruitful exchanges that deal with pressing topics such as belonging and uprooting, connection and alienation, all surrounding central ideas of human strength and vulnerability. As seems to be a constant in her work, Manuela Palacios succeeds in adding to our imagination. She has managed to delicately thread together an exceptionally rich volume in which to anchor ourselves, however temporarily.

Simon Lewis

THE GOOD ROOM

I heard Mozart wafting from the sitting room
and remembered it from school, sprinted in
to share the story with my father. He was sitting
on the sofa with a tape recorder, red button down
and he glanced up, growled at me to get out.
Months later, I found him in there sobbing
in his palms after he lost his job, asking again
and again, what he was going to do as my mother
petted the anaglypta wallpaper instead of his skin.

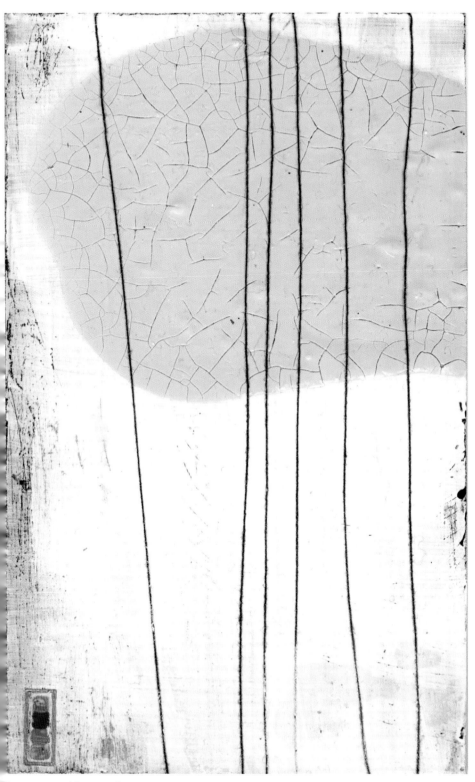

'Iconic IV' by **Aisling Conroy**
   Acrylic and nylon thread on board, 20 x 13 cm

'The Border V, R205 Cavan/Fermanagh' by **David Fox**
Oil on board, 30 x 40 cm

'Bushy Park III'
by **Paul James Kearney**
Analogue drawing on
Fabriano paper, 30 x 40 cm

'House Work, Wife, Woman, no 1' by **Vicky Smith**
Digital photographic print on photo archival Somerset paper,
45 x 60 cm (Edition 1/1)

from 'Silence' by **Sheila Naughton**
Watercolour and mineral pigment on Arches paper, 75.5 x 90 cm

All of the images in this issue are from the Associate Gallery Artists (the AGA gro
of the Olivier Cornet Gallery, 3 Great Denmark Street (off Parnell Square), Dubli

www.oliviercornetgallery.com/#/the-aga-group/4593014090

Carol Caffrey

SANDHYA KAL

A child's lone sandal capsized on
the just-gone-to-bed-still-messy floor,
an empty mug of tea left in the sink for morning,
the last parting streak of sunlight as it hangs
on to the edge of day – then. Then it was
you kept your promise and came back to me at last.

Then, in that in-between hour where
we hold our breath as night unrolls
across the earth, the interval where nothing
happens but everything might, that moment where
wakeful mind surrenders to the grace of sleep –

– then. You slipped between that sphere and this.
Your arms were tangible around me
and there was not a particle of space between us
as we hugged each other fiercely for so long, so long.
I stood within the dream and outside it;
knew the dream for dream and actuality,
felt the imprint of your face on mine
the next day and the next,
heard all the words we'd longed to say
resounding in the silence.

Note: *Sandhya kal* is a Hindu term for transition,
the period that joins darkness to light

Gillian Somerville-Large

LAZY BED

When the wind rose again
He threw down his spade
And left the neat rotting harvest.

Sometimes in Boston
He remembered seagulls
Crying about hunger
And the beauty of misery;

Mist-stroked snow-streaked Mweelrea;
Rain in strings over Clare Island
Orange sun sinking among
Lavender and salmon clouds,
Sea changing from ink to pewter
Surf reclaiming waning sand.

Grass quilts his labour,
Preserves felt stripes
Below Tullabawn.

Samuel Green

DITCH BOUQUET, INIS MÓR
  – for Sally

I am hiking west across the karst
toward the old ring fort on the highest
western cliffs a mile & a quarter
away. It's a grey day: grey skies, a raised
grey sea beyond, grey-feathered birds
gliding above stone blocks the colour
of petrified smoke like salt licks shaped
by the slow tongues of rain & wind. From
a long gryke – crack in the limestone –
I pick out crane's bill with its subtle
magenta. At the edge of a shallow
grass bowl comes the blue of harebell,
the purple of tufted vetch. I count seven
shells from sea snails in a clump of eyebright
thrown up by waves in winter, though it's two
hundred sheer feet to the water. Beside a stile
in a rock wall, the spare blooms of thrift,
or sea pink, the deep red of hanging fuchsias
with their multiple clappers. There is a gruff
music in the loose slabs of the clint, a grind
& grunt beneath the feet. Saxifrage, rock breaker,
must hum a slow version of that to itself.
Across a drainage ditch, the white of meadowsweet –
milk curdler – then a scattering of yellow bedstraw
& loosestrife. Last, in a small bite of meadow
by the gate that opens to the main path rising
to the fort is a dazzling of ox-eye daisies
& a single patch of late-blooming cowslip
offering its deep yellow cups. Imagine me standing
at a sort of altar in the inner ring of stone
walls raised 4000 years ago on the sea
cliffs. I lay my offering down on the side
that weather does not love, as though
it matters they were gathered & arranged
from all that racked & ragged grey, as though
I actually picked each flower I named.

Eriko Tsugawa-Madden

PAGE TURNER

Each time I reach the last line
My mother's hand turns the page like a score turner.
I stop reading and watch an old freckled hand.
The blue veins raised through the thinned skin,
Branching out until they fade away.
The knuckles, stiff and bent like a snake slough.
Familiar terrain.
These are my hands but so often
I can't tell these from my dead mother's.
She comes back to turn the page for me.

Adam Hanna

A DUAL ARRANGEMENT: THOMAS KINSELLA

This short interview was conducted over two meetings, as research for
a book on poetry and the law. I first spoke to Mr Kinsella in his study in
Dublin on 17 August 2017, and sent him my notes shortly afterwards. This
is a transcript of his revised answers, which we recorded on 25 September
2017. I am very grateful to Mr Kinsella for taking the time to meet me, and
to Gerald Dawe and Sara O'Malley for facilitating this meeting.

AH: Could you tell me about your time in the Civil Service?

TK: My career in the Civil Service began in 1946, shortly after leaving
Secondary school. There was a false start in the University, in science.
This lasted only a little while. At the moment of indecision I was informed
that I had been successful in a Civil Service exam for Junior Executive. I
had actually forgotten I had taken the exam – I had taken it very casually.
I was offered a place in the Department of Lands – the Congested
Districts Board – and worked there for some years. The work was inter-
esting, dealing with the old Ascendancy estates, and arranging for the
transfer of ownership from the – usually non-resident – landlords to the
real owners of the estates: the residents who had been there for generations.
   Early in the 1950s I moved as Junior Administrative Officer to the
Department of Finance, firstly in the Exchange Control section, dealing
with international currency matters. It is there I met the two young
Germans in 'Nightwalker'. Later, in the ordinary course of promotion,
I worked as personal secretary to TK Whitaker, the head of the Department – head in fact of the entire Civil Service. My time with him was
very valuable, observing how he managed great quantities of very
demanding matters coming from all the other Departments, getting
things in order for decision by the Minister.
   This was the contact point between the worlds of administration
and politics. Dealing with the annual budget, it was possible to see the
functioning of the entire economy. Whitaker had a great deal to do with
Ireland's recovery from the stagnation of the 1950s. He himself was a
notable person, dealing quietly with an endless flow of problems; very
pleasantly, never fussed. He was interested in poetry, especially in Irish.
We discussed my own interests occasionally. The idea for *An Duanaire*
emerged in one of our conversations: an anthology of the poetry of the
Irish-speaking generations dispossessed after Cromwell. With Seán Ó
Tuama as editor, and with my translations, we dedicated the book to
him. I know he valued this.

AH Was Charles Haughey one of the Ministers who you saw at that time?

TK: No. I had left the Service and was settled in America before Haughey was made Minister. His cartoon appearance at the end of 'Nightwalker', otherwise, would not have been advisable.

AH: Did you ever consider publishing anonymously?

TK: I considered it only once, with *Butcher's Dozen*; but after some hesitation still preferred to use my own name. I knew there would be problems. The poem had an immediate and considerable reception as a cheap pamphlet, with the audience it was meant for – the man in the street – and with a continuing effect, equally considerable, over the years. Really it changed the shape of my career: the loss, even still, of my English audience – despite the Saville Report justifying the point of view in the poem. My books still tend to go unreviewed.

AH: The novelist Colm Tóibín sees your imagination as emerging, in part, from the colonial landscape – its castles and walls and boundaries – around Wexford. Do you agree with that?

TK: The poetry is set mainly in inner-city Dublin, where I grew up, but I believe the colonial landscape in the poetry is important. Protestant Wexford was a new world to me, encountered through Eleanor and her mother's people. They were a welcoming people – but inquisitive, like myself. I was new to them – a Dublin Catholic. They were happy mainly among themselves, self-confident, accustomed to the unquestioning possession of property and land. It would have been unthinkable to them that their land was in fact mine – at a great remove: the territory of the Ui Cinnseallaigh, anglicised Hy Kinsella; a territory taken over very early in the process of colonisation. But, likewise, my arrival in modern Wexford, in Enniscorthy, gave me no feeling of belonging. It was their world now, not mine.

AH: Can I ask you about the other poets in the Irish civil service? There's an admirable tradition of poets there.

TK: I think I had better pass that: it could be difficult ...

AH: Could you say how the forms of your poems changed between, say, 1958 and 1968?

TK: I think of it now as a liberation, thanks largely to Ezra Pound. The escape from a world of established expectations into an open world where each poetic statement finds its own tone and form – which, if so required, can be just as traditional and formal as in the past.

I know the poetry has acquired a reputation for an almost wanton obscurity. This is unjustified: it is a fixed idea, that should disappear on a reading of the actual poetry. The poems, at every stage in the career, in the early books and late, are quite clear. I can see nothing obscure in 'The Laundress', '38 Phoenix Street', 'His Father's Hands', 'St Catherine's Clock': the list could go on. There are some difficult poems, the difficulty due to the subject matter – as in *Songs of the Psyche*, an exercise in self search. Here the central poems do need close reading if they are to communicate, but even here, the introductory verse settings are clear.

If I may refer to your own special field, the apparent obscurity is much the same in law as in poetry: the need to express something important clearly and completely, so that the content is clear to a concerned reader. There is the dead tone of the law, but the subject matter is not different, when you think about it: deep emotion, jealousy, greed, the passion of possession, opposing troubled parties, death, current concerns rooted in the past.

AH: I'm interested in the figure of Justice who appears at the end of 'Another September'.

TK: With its companion Truth, they are dream figures, returning as the speaker – waking in the first line – returns to sleep.

AH: Could you say something about your move to America?

TK: I had no plans that way. The offer from Southern Illinois University was unexpected, but the offer of complete freedom, as poet in residence, with a single lecture per year, was very tempting. I was working on *The Táin*, and not finding the necessary time. The work in the Department of Finance was very interesting, dealing with international financial matters, but the opportunity to change to a more meaningful career proved irresistible. Eleanor was extremely generous in agreeing to the move.

I finished translating *The Táin* there, and began writing a different poetry, still centred in Ireland but in a wider world. There were poetry readings around the country. Some of these ended with an invitation to change from SIU, but these were usually for faculties in creative writing. I couldn't face this, not believing creativity to be a subject for teaching; misleading for the hopeful student and the overconfident teacher. After a reading in Temple University in Philadelphia, they agreed to the idea of a course in the close reading of poetry. Later, in Temple, I designed a course on the Irish tradition, centred in Dublin, using various experts in their subjects. This dual arrangement lasted until my retirement.

Adam Hanna

THOMAS KINSELLA: THE CIVIL SERVANT-POET AT MID-CENTURY

The following text is an excerpt from a work-in-progress
entitled *Poetic Justice: Poetry and the Law in Modern Ireland*.

During a transformative period in Ireland's modern history, Thomas
Kinsella was in the crucible. From around 1960, he was private secretary
to the head of the Department of Finance, TK Whitaker, a civil servant
who has often been called 'the architect of modern Ireland'.[1] Kinsella has
said:

> My time with him was very valuable, observing how he managed great
> quantities of very demanding matters coming from all the other Depart-
> ments, getting things in order for decision by the Minister.
>
> This was the contact point between the worlds of administration and
> politics. Dealing with the annual budget, it was possible to see the func-
> tioning of the entire economy.[2]

The department where Kinsella had worked from around 1950 was pursuing a programme that involved internationalising Ireland in many ways.
These included planning for Ireland's membership of a European free
trading bloc, promoting Ireland as a destination for foreign investment
and expertise, and encouraging the creation of a new economic model for
the State. In particular, the Finance Department envisaged a shift towards
an export-based, industrial economy, something that would involve a
radical change from the centuries-old predominance of agriculture.[3]
These ideas, it was hoped, would rescue Ireland from what looked like
the real possibility of terminal economic stagnation, unemployment, and
depopulation.[4]

No exact equivalence can be drawn between the ideas that shape a
country's politics and laws and the artistic ambitions of an individual.
Indeed, John Redmond has warned at book length about the pitfalls of
yoking poems and public contexts together too readily.[5] It is
nevertheless intriguing that Kinsella's poetry and other writings from this

---

1 Michael Mays notes that *The Irish Times* gave Whitaker this title in *Nation States:
The Cultures of Irish Nationalism* (Lanham, MD: Lexington Books, 2007), p. 178.
2 Thomas Kinsella, personal interview, 17 August and 25 September, 2017.
3 Thomas Kinsella, personal interview, 17 August and 25 September, 2017.
4 Terence Brown, *Ireland: A Social and Cultural History 1922-2002* (London: Harper
Perennial, 2004), p. 241.
5 John Redmond, *Poetry and Privacy: Questioning Public Interpretations of Contemporary
British and Irish Poetry* (Bridgend: Seren Books, 2013).

time evince, like his employer the Irish State, the necessity of an international outlook and a break with tradition so powerfully.

Kinsella is part of a tradition of poets in the Irish civil service that is older than the State itself. Prominent members include the modernist and former Land Commission employee Thomas MacGreevy (b. 1893), and the Customs and Excise official Dennis O'Driscoll (b. 1954). Between these two were the neo-revivalist Customs and Excise official Padraic Fallon (b. 1905), and the diplomats Denis Devlin (b. 1908) and Valentin Iremonger (b. 1918). Kinsella himself (b. 1928) joined the Land Commission in 1946, before moving to the Finance Department in the early 1950s. It is only possible to speculate on why so many poets have worked as civil servants, but it is perhaps related to the fact that, in the mid-century, with emigration high and secure jobs hard to come by, the civil service could take their pick of talented candidates.[6]

However, once employed, not all civil-servant writers were treated equally: all the poets listed above published under their own names, while many prose writers (including Conor Cruise O'Brien, John Girvan and, famously, the satirist known to the civil service as Brian Ó Nualláin) published under pseudonyms.[7] Just as poetry was less likely to fall foul of the censorship regime than other kinds of writing, poets in the civil service were granted a freedom to publish under their own names that distinguished them from other kinds of writers.[8] The indulgence that was shown to poets was perhaps born of respect for the art form and, perhaps, out of knowledge of its limited readership.

Through Kinsella's poetry, as through Brian Ó Nualláin's pseudonymously-published prose, readers are able to see the developing lineaments of mid-century Irish bureaucratic modernity. In particular, the focus on order in Kinsella's work and the ways of doing things that held sway in the mid-century civil service seem linked. (Kinsella remarked, in

---

6 Gary Murphy writes of mid-century civil service recruitment in *In Search of the Promised Land: The Politics of Post-War Ireland* (Cork: Mercier Press, 2009). He notes that the civil servant Todd Andrews complained that want of opportunities in industry in the new State meant that too many talented people were going into the civil service (p. 128).

7 Bryan Fanning has written, in *The Quest for Modern Ireland: The Battle of Ideas, 1912-1986* (Dublin: Irish Academic Press, 2008), of the restricted latitude granted to prose writers in the civil service, at least in the mid-twentieth century (p. 193). It is intriguing to compare these restrictions on prose writers to the freedom granted to Kinsella. When he found his work on the *Táin* was not progressing, Whitaker enabled him to take a year's leave of absence and Kinsella, perhaps by way of thanks, later dedicated his and Seán Ó Tuama's 1981 anthology *An Duanaire, 1600-1900: Poems of the Dispossessed*, to him.

8 John Goodby writes that poetry was 'rarely a target' of the censors in *Irish Poetry: From Stillness into History* (Manchester: Manchester University Press, 2000), p. 19.

informal comments made before the interview published in this issue of *PIR*, that his way of moving work from the left to the right of his desk has its origins in civil service practice). The insistence on method and orderliness of the early Irish civil service became famous, or perhaps notorious. Justin Quinn has pointed out, in the decades that followed 1922, 'the patriotic heroism of the Republic was transformed into bureaucratic zeal'.[9] Michael Hartnett made the same point, but with a greater degree of asperity, noting that the foundation of the Free State encouraged 'the noble art / of writing forms in triplicate' and, ultimately, ushered in a dream of an orderly, bureaucratic nirvana: 'we entered the Irish paradise / Of files and paper-clips', he wrote regretfully in *A Farewell to English* (1975).[10] It is not fanciful to connect the civil service's famed devotion to order with the preoccupation with order and method that runs through Kinsella's work.

This ideal of order, which was fostered in Kinsella by his time in the civil service, is complicated in his imagination by its associations with Victorian colonial governance in Ireland. As he wrote in a note that preceded his volume *Nightwalker* (1968), 'Victoria was the proximate parent of the New Ireland'.[11] The words 'the New Ireland', which the speaker of the eponymous poem 'Nightwalker' sees in capitalised form on a discarded paper, underwent one of their periodic revivals in the early 1960s. The phrase had a special resonance for Kinsella, as it was the title of a 1966 speech (produced in book form in the same year), by his former mentor, TK Whitaker. Whitaker's speech, *The New Ireland: Its Progress, Problems and Aspirations*, was delivered in Brussels in May 1966. This speech set out for a European audience the ideals of free trade and industrialisation that were first propagated in his *Programme for Economic Expansion* (1958). However, the words 'the New Ireland' suggested something broader than the economic reforms advocated by Whitaker: they pointed to a more generally international outlook, the beginnings of youth culture and new forms of mass entertainment, and the loosening hold of the traditional narratives of nationalism and religion on Irish life.[12] In short, it meant the stirrings of a society moving away from the preoccupations of its own dominant, ex-revolutionary generation.

Kinsella's surprising ascription of the creation of the 'New Ireland', at least in part, to the Queen-Empress, demands a very different narrative

---

9 Justin Quinn, *The Cambridge Introduction to Modern Irish Poetry* (Cambridge: Cambridge University Press, 2008), p. 100.

10 Michael Hartnett, 'A Farewell to English', *A Farewell to English, and Other Poems* (Dublin: The Gallery Press, 1975), p. 33.

11 Kinsella, quoted by Andrew Fitzsimons in 'The Sea of Disappointment: Thomas Kinsella's "Nightwalker" and the New Ireland', *Irish University Review*, 36.2 (autumn – winter, 2006), 335-352 (p. 347).

12 Something of the buoyancy of this period is communicated in Fergal Tobin's *The Best of Decades: Ireland in the Nineteen Sixties* (Dublin: Gill & Macmillan, 1984).

of the development of modern Ireland to any received account, however. His 'Nightwalker' suggests the centrality of Victorian ideals to the new State's civil service and, by extension, the new State itself:

> The Blessed Virgin smiles from her pedestal
> Like young Victoria. Celibates, adolescents,
> We make our vows to God and Ireland thankful
> that by our studies here they may not lack
> Civil Servants in a state of grace.[13]

In these lines there is a hint that the expected religious devotion of the novice-like cohort of new civil servants is of a piece with the Victorian imperial mission that would have been inculcated in an earlier, pre-independence generation of Ireland's administrators. Kinsella's idea of the lineal descent of the present-day Irish State from Victoria is an oddly countercultural one, particularly in the light of the famine with which she is often associated in popular memory.

However, the continuity of the professional civil service founded in Victorian times after the foundation of the Free State has been widely noted by historians and cultural critics, including by the historian JJ Lee, who wrote that 'Irish public administration closely and consciously imitated the English model'.[14] Joseph Brooker, similarly, describes the decades after independence as ones in which 'a rhetoric of national renewal was accompanied by the persistence of pre-revolutionary processes and institutions'.[15] Queen Victoria's appearance in the poem in association with the new recruits to the civil service suggests Kinsella's consciousness of the persistent shaping power of colonial ideas and procedures in the new State.

A note Kinsella made as he prepared 'Nightwalker' shows that he saw the survival of the same 'Victorian' ideals that he apprehended in the civil service in himself:

> Today the <u>positiveness</u> of the Victorian mind survives in Ireland (in me
> ...) after the catastrophes of W.W. II & Hiroshima. And who will say
> this is not an enrichment, rather than an impoverishment? To be able to
> face the contemporary world, with the positiveness (marginal, yet there)
> of commitment to structure, meaning, purpose, giving, maybe, a means
> of dealing with a monster of formlessness & malignity.[16]

---

13 Kinsella, 'Nightwalker', *Collected Poems* (Manchester: Carcanet Press, 2001), p. 82.
14 JJ Lee, quoted in Joseph Brooker, '"Estopped by Grand Playsaunce": Flann O'Brien's Post-Colonial Lore', in Patrick Hanafin, Adam Gearey and Joseph Brooker, eds, *Law and Literature* (Oxford: Blackwell Publishing, 2004), pp. 15-37 (p. 19).
15 Brooker, p. 22.
16 Kinsella, quoted Fitzsimons, p. 347.

In pondering the value of his 'Victorian' qualities to a world ravaged by war and nihilism, Kinsella is imagining a very specialised form of Irish export. The countercultural nature of his ideas is clear from this passage. The idea that Ireland's people were suited by their history to offer illumination to a benighted world was a common trope at the time Kinsella wrote the above note, but the people who used it tended to focus less on Victorian Ireland and more on the Christian golden age of the seventh to the ninth centuries.[17] The fact that the author of *Butcher's Dozen* (1972) and many translations from Irish focuses on the restorative potential of his own 'Victorian mind' suggests the complex cultural dynamics at work in Kinsella's imagination. The tense and tortuous relationship with the past that is such an element of Kinsella's writing is something he apprehended in the Irish State, as well as in himself.

17 This era was extolled by William Cosgrave and Eamon de Valera, for example, at different times in the Free State's history: Michael Kennedy, *Ireland and the League of Nations, 1919-46: International Relations, Diplomacy and Politics* (Dublin: Irish Academic Press, 1996), p. 47; Tim Pat Coogan, *Ireland in the Twentieth Century* (London: Arrow Books, 2004), p. 427.

Neil Young

A SHANKILL MANTEL

Each back-to-back had one as its shrine
and matriarch as guardian who sheened
its photo-gallery as if to neglect
just one day's dust would be a betrayal. She was
the keeper of myths the wars leaked out
down every narrowed lane; she was
the one who tuned or hardened hearts
to extremities; the insulator to gluts of grief.

A brother's, father's and uncle's coats
still hung beneath the stairwell. Though they
could never return to shoulder them
normality draped from those old pegs
as surely as if the Good Lord had ordained it so.
All outside might change to reds and blues
of a louder lens, but this world
had the certainty of date-stamped monochrome.

Each day as the kitchen clock struck seven
she'd kneel to scrape the grate
and spruce the uniforms and smiles
that kept un-ageing kind expression
in the aspic of their last going-away.
Hushed talk and jokes could be overheard from the hall;
mementoes – buttons, badges, stubs
of dance-hall tickets – she kept in a childhood biscuit tin.
At supper-time, as coals glowed low,
she'd smarten the picture-frames as if
to brush the hairs off dead men's suits
and parade-wear epaulettes.
They would be there to greet her
again after breakfast; she would be there
in her apron, with tinder, wax and cloth.

Carrie Etter

Sometimes I explain home   as a list:
a cardinal's flash of red   against snow
the prairie's flatness   green stalks rising
a milkweed pod   its fit in the palm
      fat and taut with tufted seeds

Sometimes I explain home   by the way I speak
a surely brightening face   and the most banal
recollections   urgently offered

Sometimes I explain home   by drawing out the syllables
      Ill   *lih*   *noy*
and reclining   in the breadth   the breath of it

Neil Curry

VIRGINIA WOOLF ON SELF-DOUBT

What if I were to walk down to the lake
One evening, and chanced upon my parents
Standing there, and bearing my entire
Life in my arms I were to say to them,
"This, this is what I made of it."? What then,
I wonder, as I unwrapped the bundle,
Would I have to show them? Words, yes, words,
Far too many for them to bother with,
The friendship of some people of distinction,
A husband I had been such a trial to
And ... and ... but what if Father were to turn
To me, raise the severeness of his eyebrows,
And ask, "Is this it, Virginia? Is this it?"

Johnston Kirkpatrick

OLD GOAT

Why doesn't it make a run for it,
the goat, stuck there,
take to the road and go for it,
pull the stake out of the ground
and away, or gnaw
through the rope that ties it
to the patch of grass between
the black road and the white river.

So far the word *it* in these lines
replaces *goat* and *freedom*
in different places.
It is such a feeble easy word,
a lexical convenience,
lacks substance, adds nothing.

The goat too for long periods
just stands there, does nothing
but look at tedious traffic
instead of making a burst for it,
for freedom and meaning,
for connotations of goat
is what I want to say.
This goat is deprived
of its connotations.

Howard Wright

MULLAHEAD

Flattened pennies face-up on the railtrack,
a coordinate, its arabesque continuing behind
corrugated outbuildings and millipede pipes,
vast cold sheds, the tiny insect rasp of sawing.
Sump oil leaking from tyre-and-plastic mounds.
A muck-spreader abandoned askew
on heavy banks, the grumbling cattle avoiding
such contours civility itself, the heavens,
the clouds, the bronze of armour, grieves
and pauldrons, pierced, punctured and flaunted
like flush Elizabethans, then Jacobeans
who made the maps. Where three rivers meet,
Georgian coins scatter on the soft bed,
all or nothing staked in the gambling-den
under a bridge, business meeting pleasure
and kingfishers beside the plantation fields
where new engines get a turn on warm evenings.
Builder's rubbish fly-tipped on down slopes,
shotguns blast open skies above big houses
taking the sun like lonely, but fully-capable,
widows needing their roots done. Windows,
dead eyes glazed over between blackened yews.

Philip Coleman

'STOPPING ONLY AT THE ANTARCTIC': IRISH POETRY IN THE
GLOBAL MARKETPLACE

Edited by David Wheatley, *The Wake Forest Series of Irish Poetry, Volume
4: Trevor Joyce, Aidan Mathews, Peter McDonald, Ailbhe Darcy and Ailbhe Ní
Ghearbhuigh* (Wake Forest University Press, 2017), $19.95.
Edited by Jefferson Holdridge and Brian Ó Conchubhair, *Post-Ireland?
Essays on Contemporary Irish Poetry* (Wake Forest University Press, 2017),
$29.95.

Happy the Professor of English assigned the task of teaching a course on
contemporary Irish poetry at a liberal arts College in the United States in
2018! Her students can have all their course material provided – primary
and secondary – in two handsomely produced paperback volumes for
under fifty dollars! (That's about €40 on this side of the Atlantic, by
current exchange rates). Throw in another $50 – there's a 30% discount to
be had online – and they'll be able to buy all four volumes published to
date in Wake Forest University Press's *Irish Poetry* series: volumes 1 and
2, edited by Jefferson Holdridge (published in 2005 and 2010); volume 3,
edited by Conor O'Callaghan (published in 2013); and volume 4, the latest
instalment, edited by David Wheatley. Contemporary Irish Poetry 101,
starting this Fall on a campus near you. Reading List sorted.
　　Does this sound cynical? That is not the intention. It addresses one of
the most difficult problems faced by professors and teachers of literature,
and especially those who wish to focus on contemporary writing. Over
the course of a twelve-week term, say, one cannot really expect students
to buy a dozen separate volumes of poetry, not least because of the cost
involved but also because most bookshops – even the best of them –
have fairly limited selections of contemporary poetry on offer. There is
also the question of which volume by an author one should teach, and
what to do about the rest of their work, which may not even be in print.
Although the practice is legally complex, in terms of copyright law, many
lecturers prepare handouts of photocopied material, often drawn from
their own private libraries, and make these available online or in hard
copy to their students. University libraries rarely hold more than one
copy of a particular volume of contemporary poetry, but even when they
do their resources are such that they cannot cater for all of the students
all of the time, or their teachers. An easier option is to use an anthology,
where selections have already been made – usually by someone who
has a good sense of the field – and financial and legal issues are thereby
averted.

Readers can sometimes take these things for granted, but many books of poetry published in the United States every year – even by high-end presses such as Farrar, Straus and Giroux or WW Norton and Co – are not readily available in bookshops in Ireland. One can order them online, certainly, but they are generally not to be had. The same can be said about books published by some Irish presses, which are often not to be found on the shelves of bookstores across the United States. Considered within this broader context, then, in which questions of economics and pedagogical utility are very much a part of the picture, Wake Forest University Press has done a remarkable job over the last four decades, since it was founded in 1975, largely through the efforts of literary critic Dillon Johnston and, more recently, Jefferson Holdridge. WFU Press has gone from strength to strength in recent years and they publish many of the most significant voices in contemporary Irish poetry – Leontia Flynn, Caitríona O'Reilly, Peter Sirr, and others – as well as several major figures from the last century such as Denis Devlin, John Montague, and Richard Murphy. As Helen Vendler has put it, 'through Wake Forest University Press, Ireland comes to America'.

Vendler is right, of course, but anthologies do have principles of selection and exclusion, and looking back over the volumes of Irish poetry published under the auspices of the Wake Forest Series to date, one must ask questions not only about the individual poets chosen but also about the editors assigned to each volume. Interestingly, the two most recent volumes (3 and 4) are edited by Wake Forest poets, but all of the editors have been male and only seven of the twenty poets represented across the four volumes have been women. This imbalance will surely be addressed in subsequent volumes – perhaps the next four will be edited by women – but it is hard not to object to the fact that only one woman was included in the third volume, for example. While the volumes seem to be striving for representativeness in other ways – this is particularly evident in David Wheatley's selection – it is clear that the version of 'Ireland' (or 'Irish poetry') that 'comes to America' through the Wake Forest Series represents a particular kind of contemporary poetic production. This is born out of what Ailbhe Darcy, in an essay included in *Post-Ireland?*, calls a 'modern Irish tradition [that] presents poetry as a bardic craft to be mastered'. Everything about the Wake Forest series volumes, from the Patrick Scott designs on the covers to the combination of Ariston, Eurostile, and Trinité fonts inside, reinforces this impression of modern and contemporary Irish poetry operating under the sign of the Yeatsian 'well-made' tradition.

David Wheatley's selection of poets for the fourth volume in the Wake Forest Series gives this tendency a bit of a shake by beginning with work by Trevor Joyce, a poet whose work 'reconnect[s] Irish poetry with its long and fearless *avant-garde* traditions', as Wheatley puts it in the essay that prefaces Joyce's poems. Wheatley's essays provide detailed, scholarly accounts of his selected poets' careers, highlighting important contextual, thematic, and formal concerns for each of the five poets discussed in his volume, together with endnotes and suggestions for further reading. All of this reinforces the sense of the book's usefulness for academic audiences – students and professors will find these materials particularly helpful – but it also has a polemical point that is bound up with a desire to break down the barriers that have often been perceived between so-called 'mainstream' Irish poetry and its 'experimental' other. Wheatley makes a case for Joyce as a poet whose work 'is also very much a poetry for the here and now, for readers of Seamus Heaney and the *avant-garde*, Irish and non-Irish alike', but in relation to the other poets included across the volumes of the Wake Forest Series to date, Joyce clearly does not belong in the same line of development. In a way, Wheatley's collapsing of the categories of 'mainstream' and '*avant-garde*' by comparing Joyce to Heaney – notwithstanding the fact that it is a comparison prompted by a comment made by Joyce himself – merely serves to subsume Joyce's work into the 'well-made' tradition that is, finally, the hallmark of the Wake Forest poem, just as it is for poetry published by The Gallery Press, for example, in Ireland. This is not to de-value the work of these presses in themselves, nor is it to say that poems should not be 'well-made', but it is to call attention to the ways in which poetic culture creates and re-creates systems of critical and aesthetic value through the medium of publication in itself. This process becomes especially evident, and prob-lematic, when works are selected and re-packaged for the purposes of anthological consumption.

Wheatley's Wake Forest volume contains many brilliant individual poems and, in fairness to the editor, they represent a wide variety of poetic styles and practices. This is to be expected from a poet whose own work is fantastically open-minded when it comes to questions of language and form, as the work in his most recent collection, *The President of Planet Earth* (Carcanet Press, 2018), attests. Joyce's inclusion in the volume is related to Wheatley's contention that 'Irish experimental poetry is as little known among foreign experimental poets […] as it is in Ireland', but this is dubious and really only reflects a mainstream critical view of Irish poetic experimentalism. Joyce, along with other poets com-monly associated with the contemporary Irish poetic '*avant-garde*' such as Maurice Scully, Catherine Walsh, and Billy Mills, has been widely regarded and anthologised in recent years in the United Kingdom and the United States. Wheatley quotes JCC Mays's claim, from an essay pub-lished in 1990, that '[t]here are a lot of writers but they are all the same sort' – castigating Irish readers for not recognising Joyce's genius. One possible consequence of Wheatley's presentation of Joyce in the Wake Forest series, however, is that readers might not really appreciate *why* he is different, in fundamental ways, from the other poets with whom he is here assembled. Joyce's working methods alone, as well as his interest in collaboration, create challenges in reading his work that are not given sufficient attention in Wheatley's selection.

These difficulties are not unique to the anthologising of Trevor Joyce's work. Once a poet's work is included in an anthology of any kind it becomes a part of a new canonical formation and this has consequences in terms of how poetry is taught, critically received, reviewed, and marketed. Anthologisation is also a form of advocacy, an opportunity for an editor to express a set of personal preferences and endorsements. This is one of the reasons why they are often also so contentious: why has the editor included X but not Y, and what about the largely overlooked and critically neglected Z? One could be at this until the cows come home, but with regard to Wheatley's volume for the Wake Forest Series, it has to be said that the editor has done his bit for broad church representativeness. Joyce's *avant-garde* experimentalism – best represented here by pieces such as 'The Net' and 'De Iron Trote' – is placed alongside poems by Aidan Mathews and Peter McDonald that advance and problematize perceptions of the Irish Catholic lyric and the 'Northern-Irish poem', respectively. Mathews' 'visionary Catholicism' is illustrated by many poems in the selection – most poignantly perhaps in 'Kyrie for a Counsellor' and 'The State of the Church' – while McDonald's poems 'The South' and 'Quis Separabit,' in particular, make original contributions to our understanding of identity in a Northern Irish context. It is in the selections of poems from the final two poets in the volume, however, that Wheatley introduces work that really seems to transcend the political and cultural hang-ups of the last century. Introducing Ailbhe Darcy as a poet of 'the post-national poem', and drawing attention to Ailbhe Ní Ghearbhuigh's engagements with 'the rudiments of language' (*Buntús Cainte*), it is these poets – both women, both born in the 1980s – who represent real formal, linguistic, and thematic possibilities for Irish poetry as we progress into the twenty-first century.

Ideas of 'Ireland' persist in the work of Darcy and Ní Ghearbhuigh, but neither of them is encumbered by the formal or ideological anxieties that seem, in different ways, to trouble Joyce as much as they concern Mathews and McDonald. In Darcy and Ní Ghearbhuigh's work, rather, there is a sense of freedom from what Wheatley calls the 'toxic patriarchal legacy of the mid-nineteenth century' and, one might add, the century that followed. Darcy's work – 'Unheimlich' and 'Caw Poem' are great examples – demonstrates such a refreshing openness in terms of technique that it makes reading much contemporary Irish poetry feel claustrophobic.

By the same token, Ní Ghearbhuigh's poems are like nothing else in early twenty-first century poetry written in Ireland, whether it is written in Irish or in English. In a way, her work speaks to a quest for a new language, somewhere between the body and the public sphere. As she puts it in 'Bac Seirce' / 'The Love Bind' (translated by David Wheatley):

ach i ngorm do shúl,	and I watched words swimdrown
chonac focail ar marbhshnámh.	in the blue of your eyes
I ndiaidh d'imeachta	and the world I was looking for
d'aimsíos an buafhocal.	came to me as you
	swanned out the door

Ní Ghearbhuigh's work, as Wheatley puts it, speaks to a 'buoyant cosmopolitanism' that moves 'between traditions, across a globalized map of connections, stopping only at the Antarctic'.

In their introduction to *Post-Ireland? Essays on Contemporary Irish Poetry*, Jefferson Holdridge and Brian Ó Conchubhair acknowledge what they call 'the question of the disappearance of a certain version of Ireland', while noting that 'definitions of "Ireland" and the "Irish" […] remain relevant'. Their claim is demonstrated throughout the poems of David Wheatley's selection of poems for *The Wake Forest Series of Irish Poetry, Volume 4* and, indeed, Holdridge and Ó Conchubhair refer to this anthology in their introduction, reinforcing the sense of the two books as companion volumes. Several of the poets whose work is included in earlier Wake Forest Series of Irish Poetry volumes are discussed in the essays in *Post-Ireland?* – including Colette Bryce, Conor O'Callaghan, and Caitríona O'Reilly – but the book also includes discussions of earlier figures, including Derek Mahon, Seamus Heaney, and Nuala Ní Dhomhnaill. John Dillon's essay on Ní Dhomhnaill is fascinating, especially in terms of its rich archival work, but also in the way that it explores the influence of poets ranging from John Milton to John Berryman on Ní Dhomhnaill's development. The opening up of new cultural contexts, indeed, is the greatest achievement of *Post-Ireland?* in terms of the contribution it makes to our understanding of modern and contemporary Irish poetry's development. In addition to pressing for new ways of thinking about the question of influence in relation to a poet like Ní Dhomhnaill, however, the volume also invites the possibility of an expanded rubric for thinking about 'Irish' poetry that would include, for example, the poetry of contemporary Irish-American poets such as Michael Donaghy, Campbell McGrath, and Maureen McLane. Brian Chandler's essay on these poets advances such a proposition, while the volume closes with a brilliant essay by Omaar Hena on what he calls 'Ireland's Afterlives in Global Anglophone Poetry'.

Hena concludes his essay by affirming 'Ireland's increasingly cross-cultural constitution in the present century', and he 'delight[s] to imagine how future Irish poetry will become transformed yet again to take on new voices, new idioms, and new ways of writing the complexities of being in the world'. *Post-Ireland?* succeeds in its task of advancing important critical questions – the version of 'Irish' poetry it imagines is, for the most part, expansive and progressive. It remains to be seen, however, whether the volumes to come in the Wake Forest Series of Irish Poetry will answer Hena's call for a more capacious acknowledgment and promotion of all that is exciting and new about Irish poetic production in the early decades of the twenty-first century. Volume 4 has certainly opened up new ground, especially with the work of Darcy and Ní Ghearbhuigh, but it would be good to have other forms of contemporary Irish poetic practice represented in future volumes. The vision of 'Irish poetry' Hena imagines is one that would surely include immigrant poetry of the kind included in Eva Bourke and Borbála Faragó's ground-breaking anthology *Landing Places* (The Dedalus Press, 2010), for example, as well as the work that appears from time to time in Billy Mills and Catherine Walsh's 'hardPressed Dual Poets Readers', and the hugely important movement in contemporary Irish performance poetry represented by writers and spoken-word artists such as Elaine Feeney, Stephen James Smith, Karl Parkinson, Erin Fornoff, Dave Lordan, and Raven. Anthologies can only do so much, and editors cannot be expected to read everything. If Holdridge and Ó Conchubhair are in genuine agreement with the views put forward by Hena at the end of *Post-Ireland?*, however, readers have every reason to believe the best is yet to come from the Wake Forest Series of Irish Poetry.

Louise G Cole

UNDERSTANDING POSSESSION

Whenever I see red, you are across the room
back turned to me, sycophantic wannabes
hanging on your every word, siren souls
flirting, offering such wit, charm, good looks,
expensive gifts, as if any of that matters to you.

I know it shouldn't, it shouldn't, it shouldn't turn
your head, but I long for it to be me alone to hold
your gaze, keep private those secret things said
and done, deep places explored in the soft,
sticky hours before dawn, colour-drenched kicks
they'll never know of, only speculating when hints
of me float from your paintings, serenades, poems.

They might wonder at the muse who conjures
stripes of turquoise, crushed ochre, taupe,
flings them sky high, a flock of little birds to mark
a shocking summer outburst when red poppies
snagged my vision, and I raged against sharing you,
shook out my hurt, broadcast it from high places.

Stephanie Conn

DIVING FOR SNAILS

Off the east coast of Bruny Island,
neck to toe in neoprene, a man rolls
backwards from the boat's flaked rim,
barely a splash as his body enters water.
A final slice of blue flipper and he is gone,
leaving a yellow line shifting on the surface.

Below, he skirts the ragged crevices, pushes
aside seaweed and with a deft flick of the knife
frees a single abalone from rock, as big as his hand,
and slips it swiftly into the net tied around his waist.
When it's full he untangles himself from the catch,
tugs the line, sends it up to be counted, weighed.

Later, he offers me the shallow ear-shaped shell,
its lining brilliantly iridescent, shining silver
in the sun, exterior a streaked and mottled
green. He points to the black-edged foot
to indicate the name *Blacklip* but other
words stick in my throat: gastropod,
edible, mollusc – I fling it back in.

FEATURED POET: ALICE KINSELLA

Alice Kinsella was born in Dublin in 1993, and raised in County Mayo. She did her BA at Trinity College. She describes herself as beginning to write poetry at 19. "Poetry developed as a part of my life that kept me balanced," she has said. Even so, she hesitated about publication. "If it weren't for the community of poets I found in Dublin, I don't think I'd have ever attempted publication."

She was commended in the Jonathan Swift Awards 2016. Her debut play *The Passing* was performed at both the Cruthú Arts Festival and Temple Bar Culture and Arts Festival, also in 2016.

In an article she wrote in *The Irish Times* last February, to accompany the publication of her first book, *Flower Press*, published by The Onslaught Press, she aligns her work with disclosure, with the makings of elegy: a process by which language hits grief and grief is shaped differently. "I've always been attracted to the kind of intimate poetry in which the poet bares their soul to the reader. Even within incredibly confessional poems that reveal their innermost feelings, poets are always present, in order that they can control what they offer."

An elegant ability to handle this traffic between disclosure and control is visible in these two poems. 'Hot Tub Hurricane' is a skewed and ingenious nature poem. A hurricane is coming. The leaves will be casualties. There is a frantic, tonal quality about the coming storm, in the speaker's voice. She knows she herself is already a casualty as she gets into the metaphor and shelter of the hot tub, dragging the other elements with her: 'my skin which is steaming / to join the mist that is fleeing / the storm / into the hot tub / whipped into the storm of the chlorine'.

'Dawn Chorus for the Dead' returns to elegy, modulating the sounds and silences of memory and anxiety:

> The rooks wake before day breaks
> and deliver me their cawing
> through the canopy
> cloaking Haworth cemetery.

And the speaker, as in the poems in *Flower Press*, insists on a charged private space, with every intent of persuading the reader to join her there.

– Eavan Boland

Alice Kinsella

HOT TUB HURRICANE

The storm is coming
        she's on
her way
        from the South West and

the leaves are warning
        us with their frantic desire to

lower into
        the deep heat
            of the foaming
        Jacuzzi
on the deck outside the (4 star) hotel
luxury won't wait but I'm

        staring at the sky
at the leaves
        that are quivering

that are desperate to escape
        the branches on their own terms
before the chaotic battering comes like

        the Italian beside me all
      muscles and romance

Ophelia they're calling her

O
     Oh
         Ohh
I'm feelin' ya

but I cannot stop
        looking at the leaves
           as they're falling
               onto my shoulders
                 onto the heat

of my skin which is steaming
to join the mist that is fleeing
            the storm
                      into the hot tub
whipped into the storm of the chlorine

let's go to the room where there's champagne
and warmth
           and
                and

I cannot stop watching
      the leaves

Alice Kinsella

DAWN CHORUS FOR THE DEAD

They rest until the day breaks
And the shadows flee away.

The rooks wake before day breaks
and deliver me their cawing
through the canopy
cloaking Haworth cemetery.

Parsonage windows dark
            could be sleeping
church locked overnight
            could be sleeping

            slip of cobbles under foot
clip clop clip clop
            Victorian light black mist
            streetlights like fires

            catlike I slip through shadows
tip tap slap slap
            of my footfalls

close distance

chaos peaceful in the absence
of all earthbound heartbeats
other than my own so tightly
held beneath my tongue

the bells ring welcoming
seven Sunday morning
bing bong bong bing
all houses snooze still
rooks scream their panic
cries of another day –
dawn chorus for the dead –

crescendo, crescendo!

Until the shadows break
And the day flees away
They rest.

SM Kingston

IN-BETWEEN

Once an in-between girl
stepped into a narrow box
and told a man through
a wooden grille something
about herself. She was unsure
what she was saying – things
were changing – yet knew
she must be truthful
if this was to work,
if she were to emerge,
as before, fragrant with
forgiveness and prayer.

That day she forgot
the prayers and missed
her step as she left the box
to move from the church
into light so bright it pierced
her eyes. She almost
didn't recognise where she
was or who she was,
tramping home in the glaring
sun, wearing the dark indelible
blaze of words hissed back
through the grille.

"The old men of the street
wouldn't spit on you."

Michael G Casey

AN AVENUE CUTS

An avenue cuts between headstones
continues straight to door, spire, cross.
Talk of angels turns to mystery
and potential as the small white coffin,
borne in by parents, rests on the altar table
before the tabernacle, her soft toys
for company on her first and last journey.
Her songs and nursery rhymes are played –
Mary Mary Quite Contrary, Twinkle Twinkle
Little Star How I Wonder What You Are ...
Time's arrow stopped suddenly in flight;
and then a curtain is silently drawn. Parents
hesitate, turn to leave, empty-handed, alone.
Her life ended when snowdrops came.

Paul McMahon

GHOST-BIRD
   – for Kieran McMahon

The feathers
of a snatched bird

still in the shape
of its living form

floating in the air
like the exhaled breath

of an invisible
        breather

        *

the last shadow

cast the moment
the bird was taken,

showing
its presence,

its absence.

Seán Hewitt

NOT SIMPLE OR PRETTY

Tara Bergin, *The Tragic Death of Eleanor Marx* (Carcanet Press, 2017), £9.99.
Andrew Jamison, *Stay* (The Gallery Press, 2017), €11.95.
Conor O'Callaghan, *Live Streaming* (The Gallery Press, 2017), €11.95.

The planchette on the cover of Tara Bergin's much-anticipated second
collection, *The Tragic Death of Eleanor Marx*, along with the small illustra-
tions of women and spirits at Ouija boards that sit in the corners, suggest
the aloofness with which Bergin herself stands behind her own poems,
creating masks and voices, using found texts and stories, in repeated acts
of poetic mediumship and invention. At the heart of the book is the
suicide in 1898 of Eleanor Marx, sociologist, daughter of Karl Marx, and
first translator of *Madame Bovary* into English. After finding that her
partner, Edward Aveling, had secretly married a young actress, Eleanor
changed into her favourite summer dress and then killed herself using
the same poison as that used by Emma Bovary in Flaubert's novel. In this
book, Tara Bergin invokes the voices of Karl Marx's daughters, Edward
Aveling, and the characters from *Madame Bovary*, and she approaches
her major themes (love, death, grief) through what the book's epigraph
(from Marianne Moore) describes as 'illusion'.

The best poems in this collection develop on the sort of understatement and careful attention to inference that Bergin displayed in her first
book, *This Is Yarrow* (Carcanet Press, 2013). The third poem in *Eleanor
Marx*, 'The Giving Away of Emma Bovary by Several Hands', is a testament to the poet's gift for sparse but startling work, using six different
translations of a line from Madame Bovary (including one by Eleanor
Marx herself) to suggest the varieties of male control and possessiveness
over the protagonist:

> If he asks me for her I'll give her to him.
> If he asks for her, he shall have her.
> If he asks for her, I'll give her to him.
> If he asks me for her he can have her.
> If he asks me for her, I'll give him her.
> If he asks me I shall say yes.

Here, Bergin plays with the internal rhythms of the lines, building up a
chorus of voices that she then deconstructs throughout the collection,
placing both Emma Bovary and Eleanor Marx back into their own lives.

As with many of the poems in *This Is Yarrow*, many of Bergin's new
poems play with folk song, nursery rhyme rhythms, and full rhymes,

countering the menace of her voices with the unsettling apparent simplicity of her formal choices. However, *The Tragic Death of Eleanor Marx* feels occasionally to have taken the understatement of her previous work to a level where that menace, or the dark potential of the voice or scenario, can seem imperceptible. Poems like 'Faithful Henry' and 'Notes from the Arboretum', or 'Poem in Which I Am Samson and Also Delilah', manage to sustain a sense of intrigue, of the deft handling of implication which characterises 'The Giving Away of Emma Bovary by Several Hands'; however, others seem to have too little ambiguity or meaning living beyond the poem itself. The extensive notes and background information given at the back of the book show that these poems have a strong foundation, and are anchored in fascinating research, but often this work (and the poetic potential it holds) doesn't quite rise to the surface, doesn't come close enough to the poem itself to tempt us into speculation.

There are many voices, too, in Andrew Jamison's second collection, *Stay*, which follows on from his *Happy Hour* (The Gallery Press, 2012). Opening with a celebration of reading, the joy and urgency of 'trying / to read all the reading you can humanly read / in the life you have left to read it in', Jamison gives us *The Grapes of Wrath*, Joy Division, Chekhov, and an astonishing set of translations of 'lost poems' from *Feu d'artifice*, the first collection of Georges Bertrand (so lost, in fact, that not even the catalogue of the Biblothèque nationale de France seems to list a copy). A number of the poems in this collection deliver nostalgic scenes ('summer G and Ts on the balcony') or slightly hackneyed renditions of change and lost youth ('going down to where Cochrane's / ice-cream shop is now called something else'), but in the best poems Jamison probes the edges of experience, pushing what might appear to be a relatively safe lyric into more exciting territory: 'all a self is, all a county is, where they end'.

Often, the poems here take a familiar route – setting a scene, giving some description, then reaching for, or at least suggesting, a lyric epiphany – and, though some fail at this task ('Becoming a Box Set Detective', for example, never really ascends or expands into meaning), many demonstrate Jamison's ability to turn a poem in the final lines, to call us back to it, asking us to look again. In 'Bolt', for example, the speaker (walking by the Banffshire coast) sees a deer 'momentarily / snagged' in a barbed-wire fence, before turning back to the reader:

> I thought how each of us is like that animal:
> where the noise of its hooves as it bolted to the others
> was heard as far as the ear could hear,
> where it's bolting still, as far as the ear can hear.

He does this elsewhere, too, in 'Joy Division at The Haçienda' or 'Ballyhornan Beach'; however, in other instances the poems can, under a weight of nostalgia, give in too readily to the easy option, to loveliness. The translations from Georges Bertrand, like the best original poems in *Stay*, are interrogative, simple but not simplistic, understated yet probing, and show that Jamison has the ability to write poems of significant grace.

Unlike Bergin and Jamison, Conor O'Callaghan is now on his fifth collection of poetry, and has attained a mastery over form and emotion that makes his latest work, *Live Streaming*, an almost unbearable work in places. At the heart of this collection is a long poem, 'His Last Legs', that alternates between verse and prose, exploring (as other poems in the book do) the loss of the poet's father. Although grief is at centre of this collection, it is also underpinned by playfulness, and by a hard-earned optimism. The first poem, 'Grace', details the removal of the speaker's furniture from his house, notably his writing desk, and expands into a generous and warm preface, or even dedication, to the collection as a whole:

> Thanks to all those friends
> I shipped on for a song.
> Thank you rooms in shade
> that might yet prove to be
> night already happening.
> Thank you echoes echoing.
> I have more hope in me
> than I'd have ever guessed.

The intrigue of that image, the rooms in which night might already be 'happening', in which echoes might be repeating themselves, spans *Live Streaming*, which is both dedicated to 'describing matter-of-factly' this world and also suggesting the existences of alternate worlds, worlds in which the poet's father's ghost might haunt the attic room, reading *Anna Karenina* (as in 'My Father Hangs Around the House Far More'), or the wind might be a man 'who speaks in plurals, moves alone'.

Live Streaming is, in many ways, a book of hauntings, in which re-corded voices, memories, and texts, resurface to taunt and console the speaker. In 'His Last Legs', verse fragments of the poet recording him-self describing his late father's house are interspersed between scenes in which historical characters, relations, and the poet himself appear, building up a delicate and tragic account of alcoholism, grief, and the pain of mourning a strained and complex relationship. The words of St. Augustine, from his *Confessions*, are repeatedly invoked here: '*Late have I loved Thee! For behold Thou were within me, and I outside; and I sought Thee and in my unloveliness fell upon those lovely things Thou hast made.*' Early on in 'His Last Legs', O'Callaghan writes:

We owe our mother everything. Without her we would have been lost.
But you can't show grief for him. If you do, you get St. Augustine: Late
have I loved thee!

There is nowhere to put grief. I leave it here, for the time being, in whatever form.

This, of course, belies the care and precision, the playfulness and intelligence of these deeply-felt poems. As in Bergin and Jamison, the poetry
lies in the art of understatement. As O'Callaghan's 'Plum' suggests, 'often
poems have, / in their happening, / a truth so not simple or pretty / it
gets buried properly in gaps'.

Angela McCabe

HUMAN SCULPTURE

As he sat on the summer seat
in snow, in the middle of Belfast
I knew he was real.

Children tugged at his hair
pulled at his white cheeks,
fiddled with his ears.

I sat beside him,
touched him with reverence
through a hole in his flimsy jeans,
felt not underwear but cold skin.

I offered him a 'Fisherman's Friend.'
We both sucked the lozenges
as sleet blew horizontal across our faces.

Gabriel Rosenstock

CEO

Titeann ceo, ag sileadh go mín ar Ghleann na nGabhar.
Ní fhacadar a leithéid riamh cheana
(ó chuaigh an béaloideas i léig).

Luíonn ar nithe nach bhfuil ann níos mó
caidéal an pharóiste
cnámha linbh
lámhscríbhinní Gaeilge: aistriúchán a dhein Seán Bán an Ghleanna ar Virgil.

Titeann an ceo ar nithe nach raibh riamh ann
ar an mbaguette a iompraíonn an dealbhóir
M. Thierry Gillet tríd an mbaile
is nach baguette in aon chor é
ach go meabhraíonn a bhaile dúchais Rennes dó.

Measann duine áirithe go bhféadfaí é a ithe.
Blaiseann sí spúnóg den cheo agus í sásta leis.
Foilsíonn cúpla oideas sa pháipéar áitiúil
ceo le mil, le cnónna agus mar sin de.

Duine eile á mheas gur cheart sampla a ghlacadh den cheo
is é a chur go dtí an Rialtas
ar eagla gur bhaol don phobal é.
Nach ón Rialtas a tháinig sé an chéad lá
arsa fear eile.

Níor chuaigh éinne amach ina dhiaidh sin
go dtí gur ghlan an ceo.

Gabriel Rosenstock

FOG

Fog falls, trickling softly on Glengower.
They've never seen the likes before
(not since the death of folklore).

It settles on things no longer there
the parish pump
a baby's bones
Gaelic manuscripts: a version of Virgil
by one Seán Bán an Ghleanna.

It falls on things that never existed
on the baguette which the sculptor
M. Thierry Gillet carries through the town
and which is not a baguette at all
reminds him of home, Rennes.

Someone decides this fog can be eaten.
She tastes a teaspoon of it and is content
publishes a few recipes in the local rag
fog with honey, with nuts ... that sort of thing.

Someone else is of a mind to take a sample of said fog
and send it up to the Government
in case it's any danger to the public.
Another says, wasn't it the bloody Government that issued it in the first place.
After that, no one ventured out till the fog cleared.

Note: 'Ceo' / 'Fog' are part of a sequence from a bilingual
work in progress.

Cróna Gallagher

ACHILL 1972

On winter nights such as this
when iced air is cold as glass
and the blood of the sky a dark galactic ink,
you would take us outside in our bare feet,
point north to the heavens, and instruct.

We used whale bones for stools
as you hedgerow taught, pin-pointed the stars,
gave co-ordinates, latitudes and meridians
the mapping terms from lost shipwrecks
that lie still under rock studded seas.

We turned our faces like satellites, up
to find the warrior, to build it up from dots
until a giant of a man with rapier and holster
stood firm in Hibernian firmament.

Rivets and bolts formed an iron-age plough.
We would find the archeological remains
and dig it out of the dark so it could turn once more
the sods of night sky and a dash of startled milky way
was flung across the blackness
as seeds thrown from a sack.

Then we'd stand in our pyjamas to go inside,
one of us slightly taller than the other, slightly older.
Another, slightly smaller and younger and another again.
This human staircase stepping up towards your lofty world
and you, the rudder on our round blue planet
turning our cosmos, turning every tide.

Joe Wilkins

BACKFLIP, DUNCAN, MS

after the photograph by Brandon Thibodeaux

For the trailer's cement shoes
                                        just off plumb
in the Mississippi mud. For snaking from the underfloor
the three bore PVC that turns
                            & ten-odd inches on
turns again, like it's going somewhere
other than air.
                For the sagging co-ax, the naked copper ground,
for off in the witchgrass that augury of rot-boards that once, surely,
meant something to someone – please,
                                        anyone?
For the rope & tarp roof, the tired windows, the offset face
it all makes, perfect frown
                        of a flying boy.

For the air above,
                & the air below, the boy's shadow resting
on a ratty mattress.
                    For the mattress springs,
their every rusting curve yet bearing
so many tons of gone-by love,
                            days of ropey rain
& Delta sun, a thousand & one pops & locks,
saults & wheels, kicks & flips,
                                    & this backflip –
shake & sag of the boy's jeans, white tee whistling
around his skinny frame, arms wide,
fingers splayed –
                    he's going to land
this backflip, if he ever
lands this backflip.

Eiléan Ní Chuilleanáin

A MOVING HOUSE

The main humanities building in University College Cork, the university where I studied and still visit, is a large cruciform block built on the site of the house, now demolished, which was the official residence of the warden of the Honan Hostel. The hostel itself was a monument to various shifting currents in Irish history. It was built beside the institution known as 'the College', one of the 'godless' Queen's Colleges founded in 1845, supposed to rescue the Irish at one stroke from ignorance and sectarianism, with distinguished professors and a rule forbidding institutional allegiance to any religious group. Thus it was differentiated at once from the Church of Ireland stronghold of Trinity College Dublin, founded in 1592, and presently from the Catholic University of JH Newman and GM Hopkins, founded in 1851, also in Dublin.

Not only Catholics resisted the non-sectarian ethos. The hostel had started life as Berkeley Hall, a residence for Protestant students attending the university. Resident Protestant students declined in numbers and the hall was closed, later taken over by the Franciscan order of friars (their students attended the college), who didn't last even as long as the Berkeleyans. In 1913 a rich lady, Isabella Honan, left her money to a Catholic clergyman, Sir John O'Connell, to spend on education. He bought and refurbished the hostel, which then became a residence for Catholic male students, and built a Catholic chapel, which still stands on the grounds. The house that had been the dean of residence's, and later the friary (books stamped The Friary, St Anthony's Hall, included a complete run of Dickens), in 1915 became the warden's house, and the warden for the first time was a layman. My father, who was a professor of Irish, was appointed warden in 1949.

Most of my parents' thirty years of marriage was spent in my father's native city. For fourteen of those twenty-three years in Cork, we – my parents, my younger sister and I, presently joined by our younger brother – lived in that now vanished house. When we moved in in 1949 I was almost 7. We came from a pleasant small one-storey house on the Model Farm Road with a largish garden to front and rear. My sister lamented the change but I remember no regrets. I had always wanted a house with stairs and this one had three impressive flights. As the eldest too I felt an obligation to be positive. What was different in the new house? Apart from the size of the rooms, their number and names – the telephone room, the onion room, the attics – the doors into the hostel itself, the twenty-three apple trees in the garden?

Our old house was owned by my parents. They had moved there before I was born, when it was new; they had created the garden and we knew when certain trees had been planted and why. Moving there, they had left the old suburb of the Douglas Road, where my aunts and, for their last couple of surviving years, my grandparents lived, and I know my mother was glad to escape from the rented house that was so near his family. Wartime petrol shortages may have reduced visiting somewhat too. But as children we liked our aunts' home – they had *stairs*.

They – the three lay aunts, there were three more in convents – also had rather more, even, than was then usual, of the standard religious impedimenta of the day – the holy water fonts, vividly coloured crucifixes, votive lights, plaster statues, souvenirs from Lourdes, a big painting of the crucifixion in the main bedroom and a large portrait of the Dublin ascetic Matt Talbot over the dining table. The house was called St Joseph's: my grandmother had had seven children in under ten years, and my mother said that her devotion to St Joseph, who had just one stepchild, was a form of contraception. In our house we had a few Dürer saints and one dark monochrome carved-wood crucifix; my mother would not tolerate plaster. No wonder I became obsessed with devotional artefacts.

Our house on the Model Farm Road was called Tulach Óg, after the coronation mound of the O'Neill kings. It remains in my memory as a permeable place. We ran in the garden and hurt our knees and ran indoors to be comforted. My mother rode out on her bicycle dangling her cello. Visitors, a gardener, a regular beggarman came and went. We had nightmares and rushed into our parents' bedroom in the dark and they told us how cold we felt. The cat, Killarney Jim, dragged a rat in from the garden, took refuge under the kitchen stove and dared anyone to take it from him. My father worked on his PhD on the dining-room table and I was sent in to make him clear it away so we could have our tea. I had no sense of any difference in ownership between the parts of the house, though there was a maid's room with a maid in it, later taken over by Miss O'Neill, the nurse, who was called Miss O'Neill to make the point that she was not a maid.

That point immediately became more evident when we moved to the warden's house. It was a place of hierarchies and borders and structured visibilities. Now my father was 'the Professor' or 'the Warden' and he had a study to prove it – originally with wallpaper faked to look like dark wood panelling, which my mother soon got rid of. Now there was a maid's room reached by the back stairs, which rose from the boiler room, paused at a corridor with, originally, two maids' rooms (one was the onion room, which became a music practice room later) and a mysterious door at the end, and then after a few more steps debouched outside the drawing-room door. Miss O'Neill had a room beside ours, reached by the main stairs. Mrs Cotter came in by the day.

Neither servants nor children were to be on show at untoward times. I never saw my mother or father downstairs in that house other than fully dressed, and we learned not to appear in nightclothes and when not to appear at all. When the bishop came, Miss O'Neill kept us upstairs, and the maid brought in tea to the dining room, where the governors, chaired by the bishop, sat around the table with my father and his big minute book. Under the carpet there was a bell push so the maid could be summoned discreetly. Or on an ordinary evening there might be a student or two or three waiting to see my father in the large hall outside his study. The doors of the hostel were locked at eleven each night and anyone who wanted to stay out later had to come and ask for a key. In the rooms upstairs the furniture that came from Tulach Óg looked small and was joined by bigger, firmer sofas and extra tables.

(An effect I am suddenly aware of looking back is a change of the patterns of language. In our old house there was what felt like an easy swinging back and forth between Irish and English. Now there were extra people and extra business was being done, in English. Irish became more of an aspiration and speaking it was something one was accused of doing, or not doing – there didn't seem to be a right way of handling it. Much of this of course was just the effect of time passing. We were reading more and there were more books in English. My mother was beginning to make a career as a writer in English after publishing a couple of books in Irish. We were moved from a school that was supposed to be Irish-speaking – my father couldn't take their atrocious grammar – to a convent school where Irish was a 'subject' not a medium. And similarly we as girls were becoming more self-conscious and recoiling from strange – young and often clumsy – male presences, not wanting to be seen at a disadvantage. But the house also played its part).

The house had been a friary, it had been a Victorian dean's residence. It was of the same vintage as the convents we frequented when visiting the veiled aunts, and the same as our convent school. It registered vanished ideas about housekeeping (the bell board in the kitchen showing which bedroom had signalled) and still-active notions of the institutional roles and responsibilities of education, my father *in loco parentis*, and it broadcast a strong message about private and public spheres. Until we were old enough to have a latchkey, we children went in by the back door, through the cloakroom with the maid's bathroom, into the back of the hall. If you were a visitor you rang the front doorbell and the maid answered. There was an outside hall with a set of coloured glass panels which gave time for whoever was in the inner hall to whisk out of the way. There was a hard ornate chair in the inner hall, and the main stairs, but the hall then continued to the back of the house where you had no business unless invited to dinner.

Upstairs there was the drawing room where my mother sat and wrote every day from eleven to one – her greatest boast that she did not turn her head when the front doorbell rang. In a locked cupboard in that room was her collection of books banned by the censorship board, to which I was later to be gradually introduced. Also, the bottles of spirits and vermouth which might, in the housekeeping wisdom of the day, 'have been a temptation' to servants. In childhood I tried to construct the plan of house and hostel in my head, and the hardest part was the fact that the drawing room almost backed on to the room with the mysterious door – the door beyond the maid's room and on a level a few steps lower than the drawing room. It was locked too, because it led to the hostel storeroom, and every Monday morning my mother let herself in with her key, unlocked a door on the other side and admitted the hostel cook and kitchen maid to give out stores and menus for the week. Her privacy, which she needed to write, was hemmed in by those locked and censored spaces.

In the convents too there was a private life going on behind a hall door. As schoolgirls we glimpsed it the odd time, sent to deliver a message to a nun, admitted to a front hall that had a thus-far-and-no-further message written on the walls, and the one hard chair. Then a nun, whisking out of a parlour where she had been seeing an official visitor, or coming from the chapel, would have let down her black skirt so it flowed, whereas in the school it was worn tucked up short over a shortish grey petticoat. What a change in them – their gliding walk, their fresh looks – just because they were in one room and not another. And what was being concealed, what revealed? Were they letting on that four hundred children and teenagers were just sordid business to be concealed like the petticoat? Or were they concealing from us another, a more intense, life? And what was it like during the school holidays? In our house as in the convent, time and presences changed places.

A different sort of presence obtained in the stunningly beautiful Honan Chapel at the end of our garden. A rickety iron gate in the fence was wreathed in convolvulus, a weed the gardener couldn't control. Beyond that there was a vision in white local limestone, chastely carved to replicate the Romanesque twelfth-century Cormac's chapel on the Rock of Cashel. As my father's name was Cormac, this seemed most appropriate. While the college was not supposed to have any religious allegiance, the special pews for the president and the warden, and the special Masses on important days – though the chapel stood on the Honan land not the college's – made it clear that was a dead letter. Attending Mass in the chapel on ordinary Sundays was a privilege: you had to have an academic connection. The gate into the college was generally open; another gate onto the street was generally locked. A couple of pious ladies who lived on the street nearest to the gate were allowed in as a special favour on Sunday mornings and the gate was unlocked for them. One of them was the sister of a deceased warden, I remember.

The interior of the chapel was a surprise, full of amazing colours, after the cool white exterior – in the windows by Harry Clarke and Henry Healy, in the liturgically coded vestments, the enamelled altar vessels, and what my sister and I loved best of all, the mosaic floor which illustrated 'The song of the three children in the fiery furnace': *'Benedicite omnia opera domini domino'* ('All ye works of the Lord, bless the Lord'). So there was a mean-looking leopard sneaking up on a squirrel, there was a peacock and an eagle and a polar bear, lots of fish swimming in the river that flowed the length of the nave and a contorted sea serpent that I preferred not to look at. The windows, as we got older, received more attention. They were full of stories – St Gobnait setting her bees on the robbers (she is the patron saint of beekeepers) and the monks of St Nessan's monastery pretending to be washerwomen chatting in Latin and Greek to frighten away the learned monks of a rival monastic school who had challenged them.

Our house, like the convent school, like the space around the chapel, was a place where sacred and secular met, and the encounter was visible, even in an Ireland where normal life and Catholic religion often seemed coterminous. In spite of the visiting bishop and the Catholic foundation, in spite of the warden's special pew in the Honan Chapel, the secular was dominant. If there was no holy statue in the house, there was a mysterious document: the grant of arms to the hostel from the Ulster king of arms, framed in the study.[1] The marvellous vestments of the chapel were kept in our attic, but the chapel meant to my mother, and she passed it on to us, the flowering of Irish art with the work of the Dun Emer Guild (Kitty McCormack of the guild came to stay), of Harry Clarke, Sarah Purser's studio and Egan's of Cork.[2] My parents' republican background meant, in the 1950s, a commitment to making the Republic work, to the legal, the political and the practical. My father laboured over the accounts for the (Protestant) auditor. My mother opened the mysterious door into the storeroom and checked the supplies of jam and tinned fruit; she lifted the telephone, and a string of vans and messenger boys delivered fresh food and sheets and towels, dispatched by the merchants and Magdalen laundries of the city.

1 'Vert, in the doorway of an Irish Church or, the figure of Saint Finbarr proper, on a chief of the second, on a pale azure, between two lions passant to the dexter and the sinister respectively of the first, three antique crowns gold and For Motto Go Cum Gloire de agus O nora na hEireann.' Quoted in Catriona Mulcahy, 'The Honan Hostel', *Honan Chapel and collection online*: http://honan.ucc.ie/essays.php?essayID=6, accessed 26 Feb. 2017.
2 See Elizabeth Wincott Heckett, 'The part played by women in the making of the Honan Chapel', *Honan Chapel and collection online*: http://honan.ucc.ie/essays. php?essayID=8, accessed 26 Feb. 2017.

In term time, they ate with the students while we had meals with Miss O'Neill. In summer, we all ate together. The barriers dissolved; we played around the hostel grounds and ranged through the adjacent college, which was almost as deserted. We slept in a tent in the garden; we picked raspberries and my mother made loads of jam; we lined up the apples in rows in the attic and she made apple jelly from the windfalls.

Until I was eleven or so, the house was my way of understanding the world, its differences and boundaries, and how they were not always there. And even then, but more certainly every year in the later decade that I lived there, I knew that we were submerged in history. The date 1884 over the front door of the house, the stamped name of the friary on the books, reminded us how things had changed, and my parents occasionally reminded us that we too would have to move on, out of a house that was not really ours. In 1963 they left for Rome, and a year later I moved to Oxford; my home left me before I could leave home, and I never lived in Cork after that. Even now, the clean bright corridors and the water dispensers and committee rooms of the new building are slightly shocking, because I know there is no longer a family of children to be kept out of sight, and there will never be again.

This essay was first published in *The Vibrant House: Irish Writing and Domestic Space*, edited by Rhona Richman Kenneally and Lucy McDiarmid, and published in 2017 by Four Courts Press. Thanks to Four Courts Press and the editors for their permission to include this essay in *Poetry Ireland Review*.

For more information about the book, see
www.fourcourtspress.ie/books/2017/the-vibrant-house/.

Caitríona O'Reilly

INTIMATE IMMENSITY

Edited by Rhona Richman Kenneally and Lucy McDiarmid, *The Vibrant House: Irish Writing and Domestic Space* (Four Courts Press, 2017), €26.95.

Gaston Bachelard was surely the twentieth-century philosopher most *simpatico* towards, and most enabling of, the poetic imagination. Unlike the rebarbative, self-flagellating recursiveness of Wittgenstein's early linguistic philosophy, or the agency-denying and occasionally outright anti-poetic extremes of Derridean deconstruction, Bachelard's work, in particular *The Poetics of Space*, his ground-breaking study of the phenomenology of space in the poetic imagination, continually affirms the centrality of the poetic image to what he calls 'the speaking being's creativeness'. This quiet assertion is what has made *The Poetics of Space* inspiring not only to students of phenomenology or poetics, but also to practitioners of the discipline of poetry. Poets feel that Bachelard is that rare thing: a philosopher who is actually on their side. And in a time when not only the *theoria* of poetry, but also its *praxis* have effectively been annexed by the academy, who could not love a serious philosopher who writes thus modestly and unabashedly:

> The phenomenologist has nothing in common with the literary critic who, as has frequently been noted, judges a work that he could not create and, if we are to believe certain facile condemnations, would not want to create. A literary critic is a reader who is necessarily severe. By turning inside out like a glove an overworked complex that has become debased to the point of being part of the vocabulary of statesmen, we might say that the literary critic and the professor of rhetoric, who know-all and judge-all, readily go in for a simplex of superiority. As for me, being an addict of felicitous reading, I only read and re-read what I like.

So influential has *The Poetics of Space* become that any study of the spatial aspects of poetry (or any art practice) can scarcely avoid referring to it, and this is certainly true of *The Vibrant House: Irish Writing and Domestic Space*, a study which fruitfully combines poetry, meditations on personal domestic interiors by contemporary Irish writers, and scholarly essays on aspects of the spatial imagination in Irish writing and film. As Rhona Richman Kenneally writes in her introduction: 'Each piece of writing offers a distinctive way to approach the physicality and materiality of home through language and narrative'. The book's title – and much of its approach – is also in part inspired by Jane Bennett's *Vibrant Matter*, her

2010 study of what she terms 'thing-power', an attempt 'to give voice to a vitality intrinsic to materiality', which she further defines as 'that which refuses to dissolve completely into the milieu of human knowledge'. Particularly exemplary in this regard are the autobiographical essays by the distinguished writers Eiléan Ní Chuilleanáin, Mary Morrissy, Colette Bryce, Theo Dorgan, and Macdara Woods. These essays are meditations on the notion of home both as the nursery of consciousness on the one hand, what John Keats in a different context called 'a chamber of maiden-thought'; and a permanently introjected image of what Bachelard terms 'protected intimacy', on the other. The essays bear out the argument that it is this first experience of intimate space, the sheer materiality of it, that is the most important influence on the developing poetic imagination.

'A Moving House', Eiléan Ní Chuilleanáin's richly suggestive meditation on her 1940s Cork childhood, describes her family's occupancy of the official residence of the warden of UCC's Honan Hostel, at the time when her father, Professor Cormac Ó Chuilleanáin, held that post. Unlike the family's first house, 'a pleasant small one-story house on the Model Farm Road with a largish garden to front and rear', the warden's house 'was a place of hierarchies and borders and structured visibilities', with three flights of stairs (a feature that particularly pleased the young Ní Chuilleanáin), and servants' quarters. 'Neither servants nor children were to be on show at untoward times', Ní Chuilleanáin reflects, as she muses on the shift in consciousness engendered by her habitation of this suddenly enlarged and complicated space: 'An effect I am suddenly aware of looking back is a change of the patterns of language. In our old house there was what felt like an easy swinging back and forth between Irish and English. Now there were extra people and extra business was being done, in English. Irish became more of an aspiration and speaking it was something one was accused of doing, or not doing – there didn't seem to be a right way of handling it.' There were spaces too in this new dwelling that were definitely off-limits. Ní Chuilleanáin recalls her mother's locked cupboard, which contained 'her collection of books banned by the censorship board, to which I was later to be gradually introduced', and the locked hostel storeroom to which her mother held a key. 'Her privacy', Ní Chuilleanáin writes, 'which she needed to write, was hemmed in by those locked and censored spaces'. All these confined and proscribed zones, powerful enough to influence language itself, inevitably bring to mind the multi-plicity of locks in Ní Chuilleanáin's 'Gloss/Clós/Glas', from the scholar 'darting at locked presses, / Hunting for keys', to the final unforgettable image that quivers with intellectual and sensual excitement: 'Who is that he can hear panting on the other side? / The steam of her breath is turning the locked lock green.'

Theo Dorgan's eidetic summoning-up of his childhood home in Cork provides an interesting and vital contrast to that of Eiléan Ní

Chuilleanáin, not least in terms of social class, a theme which is elided mystifyingly often in Irish literary studies, but which *The Vibrant House* does not ignore. Dorgan recalls being one of sixteen children in a small house built by his father with five friends, and marvels at 'the human ecology of that house, the turbulent whirlpool of feeding, clothing and educating us all [...] the many miracles of watching distinct and individual personalities grow and evolve in that soviet of energies and cares. Three bedrooms, boys, girls, parents, one bathroom, one kitchen ... and one wage to feed us all.' Dorgan is also struck, in a passage that resonates past the pages of his essay and throughout the book, by the incongruousness of the word 'property' when applied to such a complex, intimately experienced reality: 'Property. How alien that word when applied to what we knew, in all its layered and clouded complexity, simply as home.' Any study of 'home' in an Irish context will have to contend with notions of 'property', of possession and dispossession, not simply in the old colonial iterations with which we are so familiar, but in ways that are perhaps less comfortable, closer to the bone. I was struck by the careful irony, not signposted at all, in this passage from Ní Chuilleanáin's 'A Moving House':

> My parents' republican background meant, in the 1950s, a commitment
> to making the Republic work, to the legal, the political and the practical.
> My father laboured over the accounts for the (Protestant) auditor. My
> mother opened the mysterious door into the storeroom and checked
> the supplies of jam and tinned fruit; she lifted the telephone, and a string
> of vans and messenger boys delivered fresh food and sheets and towels,
> dispatched by the merchants and Magdalen laundries of the city.

That last unheralded reference to Cork's Magdalen laundries serves as a salutary reminder that in this brave new Republic some animals were, and remained for a long time, more equal than others.

Colette Bryce's essay, '*Omphalos*', takes as its starting point Seamus Heaney's autobiographical essay 'Mossbawn', in which he writes of the water pump on his family smallholding: 'I would begin with the Greek word, *omphalos*, meaning the navel [...] and repeat it, *omphalos, omphalos, omphalos*, until its blunt and falling music becomes the music of somebody pumping water at the pump outside our back door.' With daring and pointed revisionism, Bryce borrows this rhythmic repetition and situates it away from Heaney's bucolic point of origin, firmly within her own experience of growing up in the city of Derry during the Troubles. To her mind, the rhythm of the word represents 'the helicopters hovering over the cityscape of my childhood, a constant part of the soundtrack of growing up. The army would use the racket of propellers to drown out speeches at Free Derry Corner. So in my mind, the blades are related to words, in opposition to our words, slicing up sentences in the wind.'

Mary Morrissy's 'Four Paintings and a Cloakroom' recalls her father's obsession with painting, through a consideration of the reproductions of Dutch masters he framed and hung on the walls of their suburban home. Morrissy lost her father at the age of 13. This is a lyrical, touching piece on that very Irish preoccupation with self-betterment through education, and an 'attempt to come to know my father through his collection of favourite paintings'.

Macdara Woods's essay, 'Liturgies of Fire and Water', contrasts the Umbrian farmhouse where he has spent much of the past thirty years with the vividly recollected Meath farmhouse of his early childhood. Woods identifies something essential about this common experience of habitation, something that is at the very least 'deep-European,' or more probably entirely transnational, absolutely universal. Encountering a display of farmyard tools at a small agricultural museum in southern France, Woods writes, 'no cutting-edge gallery in New York of Paris or London could have produced quite such a shocking rush of simultaneous recognition and distance. I did not register the names of the various instruments, but my hands automatically closed on phantom forms of them; I knew the making of them, their function and purpose.' An emphasis on making, on shaping the materiality of the landscape and domestic space, is central to 'Liturgies of Fire and Water'. This early encounter with material labour, whether it is fetching water, tending the fire, or making butter, has much to do, it is implied, with subsequent *poiesis*, or poetic making. The vibrant presence of these totemic objects also bears out many of Bennett's points about 'vital materialism' in *Vibrant Matter.*

The two main sections of the volume are linked by what the editors have termed *The Vibrant House: a Visual Essay*, comprising photographic images linked in various ways to the pieces both autobiographical and scholarly. There are images of, among others, the beautiful nave of Honan Chapel referred to in Ní Chuilleanáin's essay, images of the interior of Morrissy's family home, and a striking shot of Seamus Heaney's sister, Anne, standing beside the famous water pump.

Tony Tracy's thoughtful piece on *Adam & Paul*, Lenny Abrahamson's first full-length feature from 2004, is concerned with the contemporary Irish experience of dispossession in a wholly urban setting. It follows the peregrinations of a pair of heroin addicts around the city during a single day (a pointedly Joycean trope, though Tracy does not make this explicit). Tracy reminds us that the film was shot around the time of the citizenship referendum, which throws into relief a highly ironic scene during which the addicts encounter a homeless Bulgarian immigrant on a public bench, and challenge him for possession of this space:

- A fucking free country it is here. I sit where I like!
- Too right a free country. OUR fuckin' country!

An additional irony is that the bench that is being quarrelled over here in such a Beckettian manner sits in front of the IFSC, that symbol of Celtic Tiger Ireland, where, as Tracy points out 'offshore companies and invisible flows of global capital do business, literally, behind their backs'.

Adam Hanna's essay, 'The Vibrancy of First Houses in the Poetry of Seamus Heaney and Derek Mahon', picks up these themes of both the oneiric houses of Gaston Bachelard, and the agency-possessing materiality of Jane Bennett's objects. His essay examines the centrality of richly resonant objects in the work of both poets, in Heaney's case that water pump (again), the Mossbawn sofa from 'A Sofa in the Forties', and the farm water bucket. Mahon's objects are urban, or more precisely suburban: porcelain, china, his mother's Dresden figurines, symbolic both of her social aspiration and 'rage for order' and also, of course, highly suggestive of both national and international conflicts. Reflecting on the importance of these first houses in the work of both poets, Hanna writes, 'in this joining of the knowledge of the adult with the experience of the child, returning to the first house is a means of asserting the continuity of the self'.

Elsewhere in the volume, there are essays by Angela Bourke on the house of Maeve Brennan's pre-emigration childhood in Ranelagh; by Lucy McDiarmid on the unconventional domestic space maintained by Molly Childers and Mary Spring Rice aboard the *Asgard*, stuffed to the gunwales with contraband guns; by Nicholas Grene on the staging of JM Synge's interiors; by Maureen O'Connor on the domestic spaces of Edna O'Brien's fiction; and by Howard Keeley on the incipient *embourgeoisement* represented by the parlour in nineteenth-century Irish fiction. In addition, the volume as a whole is bookended by two poems by Vona Groarke, whose obsession with houses and homes is one of the dominant motifs of her work. In thus combining poetry, image, personal meditation, and scholarly essay into one beautifully produced volume, *A Vibrant House* comprises a fascinating and multi-layered examination of some of the foundational images in a literature in which notions of 'home', 'property', and 'possession' can never be simply and uncomplicatedly incidental.

Róisín Sheehy

CROMÁIN

Tá mná gorma ag siúil ar shráidenna na tíre.

Thugadar leotha an Sahára, An Mhuir Chairib,
crainn pailme, cnónna cócó, dathanna an Chongó
leis an éadach mín fineálta
a bhíonn feistithe timpeall a gcromáin téagartha.
Ón slí a shiúlann siad bhraithfí go rabhadar
chomh héadrom le druid,

A dheirfiúracha
thugamar linn gleannta Cham a Lochaigh,
Locha na gComarach, Dá Chích Annan agus nochtamar
Sinn féin do chách i mBearna na Gaoithe
Ach bhí pilailiú agus clúdaíodh sinn i mbalcaisí
Plaisteacha an ospidéil.
Níor bhac an lucht leighis leis an caesarean
Gearradh na cnámha ionainn,
Bhí oiread náire ar an gcléir b'éigean dóibh
Ár gcorp truaillithe a choisreacan os comhair na haltóra,

Tá Anú, Ériu, Fódhla agus Banba ag caoineadh i ngach
cuan 's tobar fud faid na tíre.

Ní chloiseann éinne iad,
Leanaimid orainn ag plámás lena chéile
agus pictiúirí de mhnáibh den chine gheal
atá chomh fearúil leis an impireacht
a phlaoscadh ar gach suíomh idirlín.

Chím mná gorma seasta ar leac mo dhorais.

A dheirfiúracha,
Nach bhfuil sé in am go bhféachfaimís ar a chéile agus
Beatha a thabhairt do Anú, Ériu, Fódhla agus Banba.
Go gcaoinfimís an feall a déanadh orainn agus
Na focail goirt a shil ó mo mháthair chríonna
nuair a bhuail sí mo chúl agus mé i mbláth na hóige;
'Caolaigh suas tú féin'.

Lizzy Nichols

DUBLIN IS NO BEAUTIFUL CITY & THE LIVING ROOM IS NO PLACE FOR SEX

When... it is said, 'Thou shalt love thy neighbor as thyself', it is not meant, thou shalt love
him first and do good in consequence of that love, but, thou shalt do good to thy neighbor;
and this thy beneficence will engender in thee that love to mankind which is the fulness
and consummation of the inclination to do good.

– Immanuel Kant

& Arthur Guinness
lived &
died
a year apart
in both cases.

So while Kant poured his nights
away to the ink for maps
guiding man to his
good

Arthur snuck to the Liffey
by moonlight & made night's
black a permanent stain
on once clean water wasted
in running to a sea sans
purpose. He was thirsty for
better

in a city never afforded its beauty.

Would Kant say a city
finds its good in an art
museum or a factory?
Are these bones only good
for furnishing the walls of
a city's catacombs?
How did Arthur and Immanuel weasel
into our collected dreams when night
but disintegrates at tomorrow's light?

The building that after
noon knew no beauty.
White,
Modern,
Sterile. Perfect
for a med student. We did
homework & he named all the bones
buried beneath the black
ink I've sewn across my skin.

Decorated a skeleton I trust to give
me structure with Latin ornaments
before asking to kiss
the lips on their skull.
I let him

        for a couple minutes
        before I left & went
        on the evening's date,
          knowing

                Contemporary is today's date
                in the calendar.   Contemporary
                is a white building pasted
                onto a city in red brick.
        Contemporary   is two lives lain one atop
            the other in time if not (necessarily)
                    space, &
                    like how

there is no space
for bones to transcend skeletal
line drawings and dance
together in Dublin's

        bricked-up housing crisis, where
        empty living rooms blossom
        & accommodate intimacy among
        five sleeping roommates & a man
        who channels

                rivers from the sea
                into the warmth of night's blush
                  for dawn's slow draw
                at tomorrow

                Where   gagging in the shower,
                    I pull all of our black
                hairs out from the drain,
                    to try & atone for
                my small mountain of
        transgressions & demonstrate
                that I can do good too.

Mark Ward

A LIFE IN PICTURES

A room, reserved for company,
empty, with an unsupervised tv.
I remember myself as fifteen,
sixteen but was only twelve
when I watched *Stonewall*.
It wasn't a re-run. I knew
it was on, I must've planned my
good behaviour to slip out of
sight. I remember the room
feeling cavernous, unable
to contain the film I watched,
the shower scene, my reaction,
the certainty.

This riot led
to *Jackson: My Life, Your Fault*
nestled into *Queer Street* season
back when we were niche, when
Channel 4 was everything to me.
Being all of fourteen, it was another
shower scene that burned itself
into me, two men just talking with
one saying, *I'm getting married* as if
it were possible, as if boys could do
that. I wanted my reflection to seep
into the screen.

I knew every
fictional gay boy and what made them
breathless. I found the VHS in the back
of the Virgin Megastore, when media
spanned huge shops and moments
could be rewound, words mouthed
alongside, vicariously. The cashier
smiled sadly and refused to sell me
the video, rated 18 but 15 in the UK;
boys like me were legal since '93
but shouldn't get ideas, shouldn't
learn how to sway.

Others embraced
tentative fumbles with girls that
grew more serious, carnivorous,
they learned to love, to fuck,
all of it. You were suddenly
incomplete without your other
half, a girl that you didn't need,
a boy that you couldn't be, or see
outside of the tv, there was only me.
I watched *This Life*; Warren cruising
through his easy city, doing whatever,
whomever he wanted. So,

I chose not to be haunted,
merely shadowy. I agreed with off-colour
jokes, embraced every slur they threw at me
to throw them off, or I smiled *Fuck off*
despite wanting what they accused me of,
but stopping short of being the first in school
to step out from the screen and say the words
everyone knew that scorched me into silence.
I watched Nathan from *Queer as Folk* rend
the world to his will, star of his own life,
he's really doing it, going through with it,
unwilling to sit still.

I sought out thrills,
since romance wasn't on the horizon,
and being all of seventeen found them.
Falling behind the other boys, I learned
anatomy, biology, chemical reactions
where skin ignites upon contact.
Nathan, in the sequel, was doing
just that, but had grown jaded with school
by now. I wanted romance, the great love
I was promised by my fictions but suddenly,
it was graduation and I stepped into the screen.

Notes on Contributors

Faye Boland is winner of the Hanna Greally International Literary Award, 2017. She was shortlisted in 2013 for the Poetry on the Lake International Poetry Competition. Her poems have been published in *THE SHOp*, *The Galway Review*, *Skylight 47*, *The Yellow Nib*, *Orbis*, and elsewhere.

Colm Brennan, from Bray, is a writer of poetry and fiction. In 2015 he was awarded the Thomas and Ellen O'Connor Scholarship for Creative Writing, and he received an MA in Creative Writing from the University of Limerick. His stories have appeared in *The South Circular* and in *Bray Arts Journal*.

Carol Caffrey, born in Dublin, currently lives in Shropshire. Her work has appeared or is forthcoming in *Bare Fiction*, the *Fish Anthology*, *Lunch Ticket*, *Ink, Sweat & Tears*, *Dos Gatos Press,* and *The Ogham Stone*. She performs the one-woman play *Music For Dogs*, written by Paula Meehan.

Michael G Casey has published four books and numerous poems and short stories – many of them award-winning and anthologised. Six of his plays have been performed on stage, including in the Henrik Ibsen Museum, Oslo. He holds a Ph.D. from Cambridge University.

Louise G Cole won the Roscommon Poets' Prize at the 2017 Strokestown Poetry Festival, and has been published in *Crannóg*, *Skylight 47*, *Ropes*, *The Irish Times*, and in several anthologies. She was nominated for a Hennessy Award in 2015. She blogs at louisegcolewriter.wordpress.com, explaining how the 'G' in her moniker avoids unnecessary confusion with an underwear model.

Philip Coleman teaches in the School of English and is a Fellow of Trinity College Dublin. His most recent books include *John Berryman's Public Vision* (UCD Press, 2014) and, with Steve Gronert Ellerhoff, *George Saunders: Critical Essays* (Palgrave Macmillan, 2017). He is currently co-editing a volume of John Berryman's letters for Harvard University Press.

Stanley Conn grew up and lived in Belfast during the Troubles. He is now retired, but he still loves to write and see where the words take him.

Stephanie Conn's first collection, *The Woman on the Other Side*, was published by Doire Press, and was shortlisted for the Shine / Strong Award for best first collection in 2016. Her pamphlet *Copeland's Daughter*, published by Smith / Doorstep, won the Poetry Business Pamphlet Competition in 2015 / 2016. Her new collection is due out later this year.

Tim Cunningham has had two poetry collections published by Peterloo Poets, *Don Marcelino's Daughter* (2001) and *Unequal Thirds* (2006); and four further collections published by Limerick's Revival Press: *Kyrie* (2008), *Siege* (2012), *Almost Memories* (2014), and *The Lyrics to the Nightingale's Song* (2016).

Neil Curry lives in the English Lake District. His poem in this issue of *Poetry Ireland Review* is one of a book-length sequence in which he and Virginia Woolf visit each other in their respective time zones. It will be published this year by Shoestring Press under the title *On Keeping Company with Mrs Woolf.*

Katie Donovan is a poet. Her most recent collection is *Off Duty* (Bloodaxe Books, 2016).

Briege Duffaud comes from Northern Ireland, spent thirty years in France, and now lives in London. She has written short stories, newspaper and magazine articles, and book reviews, and has published two novels and a story collection. She began writing poetry last year. The poem in this issue of *Poetry Ireland Review* is her first to be accepted for publication.

Andy Eaton was born in San Diego, California. His pamphlet *Sprung Nocturne* was published by The Lifeboat Press in 2016, and his work was selected for the 2017 Ploughshares Emerging Writer's Contest in poetry. Poems also appear in, or are forthcoming from, *Copper Nickel*, *Horsethief*, and *The Yale Review.*

Carrie Etter, originally from Normal, Illinois, has lived in England since 2001, and taught at Bath Spa University since 2004. Her poem in this issue will appear in her fourth collection, *The Weather in Normal* (Seren Books, 2018).

Cróna Gallagher is an award-winning writer and artist. Her writing has appeared in *Prairie Schooner*, *The Chattahoochee Review*, *Magma*, *The Moth*, *Crannóg*, and elsewhere, and she is the recipient of a Literary Bursary from the Arts Council of Ireland. Her etchings have also been exhibited both at home and abroad, including at the RHA Dublin and RUA Belfast.

Samuel Green's most recent poetry collection is *All That Might Be Done* (Carnegie-Mellon University, 2014). In 2007 he was named by the governor as the first Poet Laureate of Washington State (2007-2009). For 15 summers he has taught a studies abroad course in Ireland as a visiting professor for Seattle University. Honours include a National Endowment for the Arts Fellowship in Poetry, and an Artist Trust Fellowship in Literature.

Adam Hanna is a Lecturer in Irish Literature at the School of English, University College Cork. He has previously taught at Trinity College Dublin, the University of Bristol, and the University of Aberdeen. His first book was *Northern Irish Poetry and Domestic Space* (Palgrave Macmillan, 2015).

Seán Hewitt won the Resurgence Prize in 2017, and his publication credits include *POETRY*, *The Poetry Review*, and *The New Statesman*. He is currently a research fellow at the School of English, Trinity College Dublin.

Özgecan Kesici was born in Germany to Kazakh-Turkish parents and now lives in Dublin's inner city. In 2015, she was a featured poet on Near FM 90.3's Poetic Lives series. Her work has appeared in the *All the Worlds Between* anthology (Yoda Press, 2017). She holds a Ph.D. in Sociology from UCD.

Leah Keane is a native of Castlerea, Co Roscommon. She is a final year student at NUI Galway, where she is studying English, German, and Creative Writing. She has studied poetry under Alvy Carragher, and was long-listed for the Over the Edge New Writer of the Year competition in 2017.

SM Kingston has published previously in *The Salmon* and *THE SHOp*, and has read at literary festivals in West Cork where she lives and works.

Alice Kinsella was born in Dublin and raised in Co Mayo. Her poetry has appeared or is forthcoming in *Banshee*, *The Lonely Crowd*, *The Irish Times*, *Best New British and Irish Poets 2018* (Eyewear Publishing), and elsewhere. Her debut, *Flower Press*, was published this year by The Onslaught Press.

Johnston Kirkpatrick has published poems in the *New Statesman*, the *Times Literary Supplement*, and *The Honest Ulsterman*. A selection of his poems, along with work from Peter McDonald and Trevor McMahon, is included in *Trio 3*, published by The Blackstaff Press.

Simon Lewis was the winner of the Hennessy Prize for Emerging Poetry, and the runner up in the Patrick Kavanagh Poetry Award, in 2015. His first collection, *Jewtown* (Doire Press, 2016), was shortlisted for the Shine/ Strong Award in 2017. See **www.simonlewis.ie**

Laura Linares is a Ph.D. candidate and Assistant Lecturer in the Department of Spanish, Portuguese, and Latin American Studies in UCC. Her project explores the approaches taken in the translation and mediation of literature from a minority/minorized culture (Galician) into the hegemonic English speaking-world.

Daniel Lusk is the author of six poetry collections, including most recently *The Shower Scene from Hamlet* (2017), as well as a memoir, *Girls I Never Married*, and other books. His genre-bending essay 'Bomb' was awarded a 2016 Pushcart Prize. His work has appeared widely in literary journals, including *New Letters*, *North American Review*, *Prairie Schooner*, *The Iowa Review*, and *Poetry*. He lives in Vermont with his wife, Irish poet Angela Patten.

Angela McCabe was the winner of the Listowel Poetry Collection Competition in 2016. Several of her prize-winning poems have appeared in anthologies and literary magazines worldwide. She writes screenplays and has made an award-winning short movie. Her third poetry book will be published later this year.

Thomas McCarthy is a former winner of the Patrick Kavanagh Award and the Alice Hunt Bartlett Prize. He is the author of nine collections of poetry and two novels. His latest collection, *Pandemonium* (Carcanet Press, 2016), was short-listed for the *Irish Times*/Poetry Now Award. He is a former editor of *Poetry Ireland Review* and the *Cork Review*.

Marion McCready lives in Argyll, Scotland. She is the author of two collections of poetry, *Tree Language* (Eyewear Publishing, 2014), and *Madame Ecosse* (Eyewear Publishing, 2017).

Paul McMahon is from Belfast. His debut chapbook, *Bourdon*, was published by Southword Editions in November 2016. His poetry awards include The Keats-Shelley, The Ballymaloe, The Nottingham, The Westport, and The Golden Pen. His poetry has appeared in *The Irish Times*, *The Threepenny Review*, *The Stinging Fly*, *Best British and Irish Poets 2018* (Eyewear Publishing), and elsewhere.

Paula Meehan was born and lives in Dublin. She was Ireland Professor of Poetry, 2013–2016. Her public lectures from the Professorship, *Imaginary Bonnets with Real Bees in Them*, are published by UCD Press. *Geomantic* (2016), her latest collection, is published by The Dedalus Press.

Julie Morrissy's debut collection – *Where, The Mile End* – is forthcoming in 2019 from BookThug (Canada). In 2016, her pamphlet *I Am Where* was shortlisted in the Saboteur Awards, and she was selected by Poetry Ireland as a 'Rising Generation' poet. Morrissy is Vice-Chancellor Research Scholar at Ulster University, where she is pursuing her Ph.D. by practice.

Travis Mossotti's latest collection, *Narcissus Americana* (University of Arkansas Press, 2018), was selected by Billy Collins as the winner of the 2018 Miller Williams Poetry Prize. Mossotti teaches at Webster University and works for Washington University in the Office of the Vice Chancellor for Research.

Lizzy Nichols, originally from the Southwestern United States, is currently an M.Phil. student at Trinity College Dublin, studying Literatures of the Americas. Her writing has previously appeared or is forthcoming in *Cardinal Sins*, *The Offbeat*, *The Tishman Review*, and elsewhere.

Eiléan Ní Chuilleanáin is an emeritus fellow of Trinity College Dublin, and the current Ireland Professor of Poetry. She has published eight collections of her poetry, the latest of which is *The Boys of Bluehill* (The Gallery Press/Wake Forest University Press, 2015).

Doireann Ní Ghríofa's most recent book is *Oighear* (Coiscéim, 2017). Among her awards are the Rooney Prize for Irish Literature and a Seamus Heaney Fellowship.

Dan O'Brien's poetry collections are *War Reporter* (CB Editions / Hanging Loose Press, 2013), *Scarsdale* (CB Editions, 2014 / Measure Press, 2015), and *New Life* (CB Editions, 2015 / Hanging Loose Press, 2016). He lives in Los Angeles.

Jimmy O'Connell, born in Dublin, is now based in Co Meath. He spent some time working in America, and has been writing for many years. Wordsonthestreet published a collection of his poetry, *Although it is Night*, in 2013, and he has read his poems in many venues across Ireland.

Ita O'Donovan was born in Cork and now lives in Clifden. Her work has been published in *Poetry Ireland Review*, *THE SHOp*, *Southword*, *Skylight 47*, and in various anthologies. She was shortlisted for *The Irish Times* Hennessy New Irish Writing Awards. In 2017 her first collection, *In Deep Time – Connemara*, was published by The Knocknarone Press.

Tony O'Dwyer's poetry has been published in *Poetry Ireland Review*, *The Stony Thursday Book*, *The Raintown Review* (US), and *The Cúirt Journal*. He was runner-up in The Patrick Kavanagh Award in 1999. His first collection, *Off Guard*, was published by Bradshaw Books in 2003. He is co-editor of *Crannóg* magazine (**www.crannogmagazine.com**).

Rugadh **Simon Ó Faoláin** i 1973 i mBaile Átha Cliath agus tógadh é in Iarthar Duibhneach. Tá trí leabhar filíochta Gaeilge foilsithe aige. I measc na ngradam atá buaite aige dá scríbhneoireacht tá Duais Glen Dimplex, Duais Strong, Duais Bhaitéar Uí Mhaicín, Duais Cholm Cille, agus Duais Foras na Gaeilge.

Stiofán Ó hIfearnáin has been published in *Comhar* and *The Stinging Fly*. A graduate of UCD (German and History), he is currently completing his teacher training at NUIG.

Caitríona O'Reilly has published three full collections of poetry with Bloodaxe Books: *The Nowhere Birds* (2001); *The Sea Cabinet* (2006); and *Geis* (2015), shortlisted for the 2016 Pigott Prize and the winner of the 2016 *Irish Times* Poetry Now Prize. She also writes literary criticism and has published some short fiction. She lives in Lincolnshire.

Ciarán O'Rourke was awarded the Lena Maguire/Cúirt New Irish Writing Award (2009), the Westport Poetry Prize (2015), and the Fish Poetry Prize (2016). A widely-published poet, his first collection is forthcoming from Irish Pages Press.

Gabriel Rosenstock, poet, tankaist, haikuist, essayist, playwright, and novelist, was born in 1949 in postcolonial Ireland. His Irish-language versions of Goan poetry appeared recently in the bilingual anthology *Goa: A Garland of Poems* (The Onslaught Press, 2017). He blogs at http://roghaghabriel.blogspot.ie/

Breda Wall Ryan's debut collection, *In A Hare's Eye* (Doire Press, 2015), was shortlisted for The Shine/Strong Award.

Fiona Sampson is Professor of Poetry at the University of Roehampton. *In Search of Mary Shelley: The Girl Who Wrote Frankenstein* is published by Profile Books, and by Pegasus Books in the US.

David Sergeant has written two collections of poetry; the most recent, *The Pronoun Utopia*, is published by Green Bottle Press.

Róisín Sheehy's debut play, *Snámh na Saoirse*, was produced by An Lab Theatre in An Daingean/Dingle, and at An Taibhdhearc, Galway, in 2017. Her poetry and prose has been published in *An tUltach*, *Cómhar*, *Feasta*, *Southword*, and broadcast on Sunday Miscellany, RTÉ Radio 1. Róisín is invigorated by dance and often weaves movement into her poetry.

Gillian Somerville-Large has had two collections of poems published by Lapwing, *Karamania* in 2011 and *Ightermurragh in the Rain* in 2013. She lives in Kilkenny with her husband, the writer Peter Somerville-Large.

Breda Spaight was selected for the Poetry Ireland Introductions Series in 2017. She was also among the poets accepted for the Cork International Poetry Festival Introductions Readings in 2018. She is featured poet in the current issue of *The Stinging Fly*.

Jessica Traynor's debut collection, *Liffey Swim* (The Dedalus Press, 2014), was shortlisted for the Strong/Shine Award. New poems in response to Jonathan Swift's *A Modest Proposal* were published by The Salvage Press in 2017. Her awards include the Ireland Chair of Poetry Bursary and Hennessy New Irish Writer of the Year. Her second collection is forthcoming later this year.

Eriko Tsugawa-Madden was born in Hokkaido in Northern Japan and moved to Ireland in 1989. She writes poems in both English and Japanese. Her first bi-lingual poetry book, *Bride of the Wind*, was published in 2013. She lives in Dublin.

Jean Tuomey, originally from Dundalk, currently lives in Castlebar. A former teacher, she trained as a writing facilitator with the National Association for Poetry Therapy in the United States, and now facilitates writing groups. She is published in *Crannóg, The Fish Anthology 2011, Stony Thursday*, and *Washing Windows? Irish Women Write Poetry* (Arlen House, 2017).

Mark Ward is from Dublin. He was Poet Laureate of *Glitterwolf* and a featured poet in the final Lingo Festival. His poems have appeared in numerous magazines and anthologies. He founded and edits *Impossible Archetype*, a journal of LGBTQ+ poetry. His chapbook, *Circumference*, is forthcoming from Finishing Line Press.

Joe Wilkins is the author of a memoir, *The Mountain and the Fathers* (2012), and three collections of poetry, including *When We Were Birds* (University of Arkansas Press, 2016). His novel, *Fall Back Down When I Die*, is forthcoming from Little, Brown and Co in 2019. He lives in western Oregon and teaches writing at Linfield College.

Howard Wright lectures at the Ulster University, Belfast. Blackstaff Press published *King of Country* in 2010. *Blue Murder*, published by Templar Press/ Iota Shots, followed in 2011. He is twice a winner of The Frogmore Prize. He was longlisted in the 2016 National Poetry Competition and shortlisted in the PBS Pamphlet 2016/17 Competition. He was also highly commended in last year's Ver Poets Open. Recent work has been published in *Cyphers* and *Blackbox Manifold*, and is due to appear in *Stand* and *Southbank Poetry*.

Neil Young hails from Belfast and now lives in Aberdeenshire, where he is co-founder of *The Poets' Republic* magazine. He has written three chapbooks: *Lagan Voices* (Scryfa, 2011), *The Parting Glass: 14 Sonnets* (Tapsalteerie, 2016), and *Jimmy Cagney's Long-Lost Kid Half-Brother* (Black Light Engine Room, 2017).